Christ Unmasked

Studies in Religion

Christ Unmasked ❖ The Meaning of *The Life of Jesus* in German Politics

Marilyn Chapin Massey

The University of North Carolina Press

Chapel Hill and London

For my daughters,
Lisa Katherine Massey
and Sarah Elizabeth Massey

Manufactured in the United States of America

Library of Congress Cataloging in Publication Data

Massey, Marilyn Chapin, 1942–
Christ unmasked.

(Studies in religion)
Bibliography: p.
Includes index.
1. Strauss, David Friedrich, 1808–1874. Das Leben Jesu. 2. Jesus Christ—Biography. 3. Christian biography—Palestine. 4. Germany—Politics and government—1806–1848. I. Title. II. Series: Studies in religion (Chapel Hill, N.C.)
BT301.S73M37 1983 232.9'01 82-8547
ISBN 0-8078-1524-1 AACR2

Contents

Preface

This search for the political meaning of *The Life of Jesus* is for me a fresh experiment in doing history. I have been motivated to undertake it by the concerns I share with feminist, black, and minority historians who seek to recover dimensions of human experience and meaning that historical traditions have excluded. One of the best of these historians, Linda Gordon, maintains that this type of historical scholarship involves membership in "a tradition several centuries old of people struggling collectively for more freedom."[1] In a sense, then, my concern with this tradition motivates my quest for the political meaning of *The Life of Jesus*. I think the text addressed the issue of "people struggling collectively for more freedom," and I have attempted to recover that meaning of the text, which the intellectual historical traditions of theology and philosophy have excluded.

Gordon also stated that "to deny our membership in this tradition is to waste precious resources."[2] I would add that to try to hide this membership in the name of some sort of historical objectivity is to continue to leave fundamental questions about history unasked. There is an essential connection between the perspectives of those who ask these radical questions and a multidisciplinary approach to the past. Historians seeking the experiences of groups about which recognized historical traditions have been silent have inevitably challenged the definition of history as a product of and belonging to those with power, the controlling subjects. To extend this challenge to intellectual history is to question its status as a product and possession of the controlling subject's, the great author's, intentions and to search for ways of uncovering ignored or repressed meanings of what are called "great ideas." At the root of both these challenges is a philosophical question about the *basis* of the long-standing identification of history with the deeds and ideas of outstanding people and the concomitant exclusion from history of others not perceived as its subjects. In Simone de Beauvoir's terms, this is the question about the foundation of the category of the "other." Why has priority been given in Western philosophical thought to the structure of a subject or self over against an object or "other"? And why has this structure, which corresponds with concepts of opposition and exclusion, predominated over one which could account for mutuality and inclusion?

In his article "Rethinking Intellectual History and Reading Texts," Dominick LaCapra points out how both the separation of historical disciplines and the norms of intellectual history are ineluctably entangled in this question. He explains that the quest for purity in knowledge, "pure fact, pure fiction, pure philosophy," and, I would add, for pure truth in religion and theology, "may be institutionalized in disciplines that organize themselves around conventions and rules that restrict language to certain uses and prohibit or sanction the attempt to raise questions that problematize these restricted uses. One of the largest of these questions is whether the quest for purity and the direct projection of analytic categories onto 'reality' are related to 'metaphysics of the proper' whereby one's own identity, propriety, or authenticity is established through the identification of a totally different 'other' or outsider who may even become a pariah or scapegoat."[3] To state it directly, the restrictive function of academic disciplines keeps aspects of human experience and meanings of "great ideas" outside the realm of the "important" or even the "real." What I hope to accomplish with this multidisciplinary experiment is to initiate a reevaluation of what is "important" and "real" about nineteenth-century Christian thought.

For the excellence of their own historical scholarship and for the encouragement they have given me to pursue the issues of this study, I want to thank Brian A. Gerrish, Hans W. Frei, and Van A. Harvey. Terry Hancock Foreman helped me immensely by reading this work in its first draft and by providing me with his own model of imaginative scholarship on Schleiermacher. I am indebted to the growing group of feminist scholars who have helped me find ways to explore the interrelationships of the aspects of culture which traditional disciplines have separated. Most of all, I thank my inimitable companion, James A. Massey, for sharing with me his brilliance, his daring, and his love.

Christ Unmasked

Introduction

The Life of Jesus, Critically Examined (1835), by David Friedrich Strauss (1808–74), is one of the most celebrated books of the nineteenth century.[1] Christian theologians hail it as the work that gave shape to the discipline of biblical criticism and that decisively articulated the question of the viability of faith in a secular age. Political and social historians consider that, by its influence on the left-wing Hegelians and Karl Marx (1818–83), the book changed the course of European and world history. Yet while its definitive roles in the history of Christian thought and in political and social history are widely acknowledged, the relationship between these roles has never been adequately explained. The purpose of this book is to provide that explanation: an explanation grounded in the political meaning of *The Life of Jesus*.

The political meaning of this famous text has been lost in the gaps separating academic disciplines—specifically, the gaps separating political, social, and intellectual history, along with that even wider divide between intellectual history and aesthetics. A trip down the blind alleys created by the divorce of disciplines can help make clear the multidisciplinary route taken here in order to locate the political meaning of *The Life of Jesus*.

The Limits of Intellectual History

Dominick LaCapra contends that "when texts are relegated to discrete disciplines they are read in an excessively reductive way."[2] This statement could not be more accurate with respect to *The Life of Jesus*. Political historians and social historians have been content to relegate the interpretation of *The Life of Jesus* to the discipline of Christian theology. Accordingly, the reading of the text has been undertaken by intellectual historians, who have relied on philosophical and theological ideas, principally those of the Hegelian philosophy.[3] Central to most of these readings are two questions: Is Strauss's concept of myth rationalistic or Hegelian? and Did Strauss understand the Hegelian philosophy of religion correctly? It is obvious that whatever the answers to these questions, they cannot provide information about the text's social and political importance. Inevitably, historians of Christian thought, like all historians who focus on systems of ideas and their transmission while ignoring or paying only slight attention to political and social history, provide a reductive reading of the text. This study contends that only when the Hegelian philosophy of religion is brought together with another type of interpretive guide can the political meaning of *The Life of Jesus* become evident.

For their part, political and social historians, to whom the particulars of the intellectual historians' discussion of Strauss's use or misuse of systems of ideas convey no political significance, focus on the fact that *The Life of Jesus* challenged Christian orthodoxy. They reduce its ideological content to the descriptive term *religious radicalism*. "Radicalism" is then used as the contentless link holding together theology and politics. Thus in political and social histories *The Life of Jesus* is usually bracketed as a "purely religious" text, which because of its attack on Christian orthodoxy served as an impetus to criticisms of religion that "later" became political.[4] The rich content of this text, which altered the history of Christian thought, is not understood as having any *direct* relation to the role of the book in altering Western social and political history.

Furthermore, the customary approaches of intellectual history to textual interpretation—and not merely its separation from sociopolitical history—hinder the discovery of the political meaning of *The Life of Jesus*. These unfruitful approaches are: the interpretation of the ideas of a text as instances of a tradition and the use of the author's intentions as the key to interpretation.

No one has exemplified more tellingly than Ferdinand Christian Baur (1792–1860), one of the first and most influential critics of *The Life of Jesus*, the loss of meaning that results from viewing it from within the parameters of a tradition. He wrote:

> If there is any book which is constructed as much as possible only on the work of predecessors, which simply summarizes a string of various investigations long ago conducted by so many others, which merely, but consistently draws the last conclusion from premises about which one had already been agreed, then it is Strauss's *Life of Jesus*—what then, in the whole work, is new and unprecedented? Where is even one assertion to be found in it that is first here put forward, and has not already been dared by other theologians whom no one can accuse of an anti-Christian direction? . . . When one considers Strauss's work *from this side* then one in fact has trouble finding it conceivable how it caused such an extraordinary sensation in its first appearance, not at all just among the uninitiated, but especially among those to whom the most of what has been said here could have been long since no secret.[5]

In this reading of *The Life of Jesus* as a transmitter of a tradition, even the external link to its political significance, its religious radicalism, is lost. The limitations of reading any text in this way are well stated by LaCapra: "[This type of] interpretation often treats [great] texts in terms that domesticate them by emphasizing their commonality with lesser works or with ordinary beliefs, desires, tensions, and values. This begs a number of crucial questions. Are great texts of special interest not in their confirmation or reflection of common concerns but—to paraphrase Nietzsche—*in the exceptional way* in which they address commonplace themes?"[6]

Customarily, historians of theological ideas have focused on an author's intentions to locate what is great or exceptional about a text. By way of intentionality, the exceptional in a text is associated with the exceptional—that is, the unique or original—in the author. This sort of approach to the greatness of *The Life of Jesus* provides no access to its political meaning. There is no path to be followed from Strauss's stated, or reconstructed, intentions to the text's political meaning. There is no evidence that Strauss intended to write a veiled political treatise or that he had any other than theological and philosophical motives in writing *The Life of Jesus*. Furthermore, the intellectual historians who use this approach and who do attempt to describe the political meaning of *The Life of Jesus* tend to read it as representative of the mildly liberal and even conservative political positions espoused by Strauss in his later life. Karl Barth's portrait of Strauss as the quintessential middle-class nineteenth-century German has been most influential in this regard.[7] Thus, explaining why and how *The Life of Jesus* had political meaning entails finding ways both of interpreting the meaning of the text which escaped the control of the author's theological and philosophical intentions and of closing the gaps between historical disciplines.

Aesthetics, Politics, and History

An analysis of the literary qualities of *The Life of Jesus* as that aspect of the text which, in a sense, stands between its ideas and its historical context is necessary to explain its political meaning.

A comparison of *The Life of Jesus* with a novel about a tragic young woman, *Wally the Skeptic* (1836),[8] written by Karl Gutzkow (1808–78) will help identify the characteristics of the text that lent a political cast to its technical theological and biblical content. Six months after this novel was published, it was censored and Gutzkow was sent to prison, convicted of threatening the social and political order with the story of Wally. Although associated with one another in the public mind, *The Life of Jesus* and *Wally the Skeptic* had no direct influence on each other. Both texts were written in Germany when their authors were in their mid-twenties, however, and thus they share a genesis in a generation.

The comparison of *The Life of Jesus* with *Wally the Skeptic* provides a focal point for reading the ideas of *The Life of Jesus* out of the cultural situation rather than through the author's intentions or through some autonomous system of ideas. Clarifying what *The Life of Jesus* had in common with this threatening novel is a step toward identifying those cultural conditions in the Germany of the 1830s shared by Strauss and Gutzkow and others of their generation. In a certain sense, placing *The Life of Jesus* together with *Wally the Skeptic*, rather than with its customary confreres in theology and philosophy, makes it just one player among others in the decades before the German revolution of 1848. But this demotion, while a necessary step in drawing intellectual and sociopolitical history closer together, is not a final one. To view a text as nothing more than a reflection of *common* cultural modes can be as reductive of a "great" text as to view it as Baur viewed *The Life of Jesus*, that is, as nothing more than a repetition of tradition. *The Life of Jesus* is a celebrated book because it did more than rehearse an intellectual tradition or mirror the times; it altered both. The comparison of the text with the contemporary novel *Wally the Skeptic* also provides the key to identifying its power of change. This key is its literary style, "the exceptional way in which it addressed commonplace themes."

LaCapra maintains that the style of a text can be more potent as a "politically subversive or contestatory force" than overt revolutionary assertions "packaged in conventional forms."[9] The comparison here of *The Life of Jesus* and *Wally the Skeptic* demonstrates that the style of the theological text was just such a force. Furthermore, as LaCapra also points out, when texts are put on trial, either in actual courts (as was *Wally the Skeptic*) or by the critical responses to it (as was *The Life of Jesus*) the power of style is repressed.

Few books have aroused either the volume or intensity of critical reaction that *The Life of Jesus* elicited. To defend it, Strauss himself and other left-wing Hegelians wrote about literary style—literary style in general and the style of *The Life of Jesus*—in articles ignored by contemporary and later theological and philosophical critics. In this study these defenses are resurrected and given the standing of astute interpretations of *The Life of Jesus*. Strauss's statements were certainly not expressions of guiding intentions—that is, they are not evidence that he consciously structured *The Life of Jesus* with the intent to form a politically subversive document. But when "on trial,"

Strauss, along with other defenders of *The Life of Jesus*, had some realization of the political power of its literary style. Paying attention to these observations, then, presents an additional guide to a political reading of the text that remains close to the historical conditions of its influence.

Two recent historical studies have contributed to this multidisciplinary undertaking. One is a history of eighteenth- and early-nineteenth-century biblical hermeneutics, *The Eclipse of Biblical Narrative*, by Hans W. Frei. In this work Frei compares the development of methods of biblical criticism with the emergence of the genre of realistic narrative in the novel, first in England and then in France, under the thesis that a significant part of the Bible, including the Gospels, belongs to the genre of realistic narrative. He contends that in Germany, where biblical hermeneutics flourished, a politically and socially determined lack of realism in letters can account for the predominance of positivist and idealist biblical hermeneutics.

The other study that influenced this work is a history of the left-wing Hegelian journal, *The Halle Yearbooks for German Science and Art*, by James A. Massey. In contrast to most studies of left-wing Hegelianism, which trace the history of ideas as expressed and transmitted by individual thinkers, Massey's work on the *Halle Yearbooks* locates the group's developing thought in the context of German culture. He shows that this journal was engaged in an elementary sociology of knowledge and that, read from this perspective, its judgments on *The Life of Jesus* can contribute to the analysis of the role of that work in the Germany of the 1830s.

Many schools of interpretation, including those of the new criticism, structuralism, post-structuralism, Critical Theory, and Marxist interpretation generally, are characterized by their turn away from the intentional subject as the source of cultural meaning. Michel Foucault's way of exposing the limits of the traditional definition of the role of the subject in history, while not directly determining the approach in this study, has most directly inspired its goals. In *The Order of Things*, Foucault asked "whether the subjects responsible for their scientific discourse are not determined in their situation, their function, their perceptive capacity, and their practical possibilities by conditions which dominate and even overwhelm them."[10] The identification of general cultural configurations that dominated Strauss and others of his generation is a central element in this explanation of the political meaning of what was intended as a theological book. But the archeological depths plumbed by Foucault in order to identify what he terms "systems of regularities" are far below the level at which answers to questions about the political meaning of *The Life of Jesus* can be found. To identify what rendered *The Life of Jesus* politically potent this study seeks to cross customary disciplinary boundaries close to the surface of culture, following historical clues rather than any single theoretical frame. Interweaving political, literary, social, and religious history, the analysis here forms a network within which the reader can recognize the idioms of German culture in the 1830s. A closer look at the text, then, reveals how *The Life of Jesus* caught up and changed certain of those idioms.

Foucault, in more recent work, has focused directly on the relationship between knowledge and power, seeking to contribute to what he calls "the insurrection of subjugated knowledges."[11] By subjugated knowledges he designates two quite different types. One is "erudite knowledge," "blocs of historical knowledge which were present but disguised within the body of functionalist and systematising theory." This type of subjugated knowledge is similar to that knowledge which is excluded by disciplinary boundaries. The second type is what Foucault calls popular (but not commonsense) knowledge, "local memories," "naive knowledges located low down on the hierarchy, beneath the required level of cognition or scientificity."[12] It is, to use his example, the knowledge of the ill person or the nurse, not the knowledge of medical science. Both types of subjugated knowledges have to do with a "historical knowledge of struggles," and thus to reach that knowledge of struggles, in Foucault's opinion, a historical method must unite erudite knowledge and popular knowledge.[13] With such a method Foucault himself directly investigates the distribution and exercise of power in modern society.

While motivated by questions about power in society and

especially the exclusion from the legitimated exercise of power of entire categories of humans, this study of *The Life of Jesus* is directly concerned with a *concept* of power, the notion of sovereignty, a publicly recognized power arrangement, implicit in the text's theological knowledge. Nevertheless, a union of erudite knowledge and a certain form of popular knowledge is considered essential to this concern. Although present here in the form of a story, Wally's knowledge is a popular knowledge, "low-ranking, unqualified," and, as she feels so acutely, an "even directly disqualified" knowledge.[14] The union of the Hegelian philosophy with *Wally the Skeptic* in interpreting *The Life of Jesus* thus ranks together Wally's naive knowledge and philosophical erudition. The divorce of those knowledges as well as the divorce of disciplines accounts for why the political meaning of *The Life of Jesus* has been lost to historians.

Chapter One ❖ Texts and Language

In 1834, Heinrich Heine (1799–1865) wrote that in order for the German people to effect social and political change like that of the French, "it [was] important at the moment to neutralize the power of religion."[1] A decade later, Marx claimed that this neutralization had taken place. He wrote, "For Germany the criticism of religion is essentially completed."[2] This criticism, which Marx, in agreement with Heine, considered to be the prerequisite of political and social criticism, and thus of actual change, began almost as soon as Heine proclaimed its necessity. It had its origins in 1835, in the south German university town Tübingen, when a young seminary instructor, David Friedrich Strauss, sent to press a lengthy, academic study of the historicity of the gospel narratives, *The Life of Jesus, Critically Examined.*

When it appeared, this book instantly evoked a "panic-stricken terror" in Germany.[3] Wolfgang Menzel (1798–1873), a popular cultural critic, raged against *The Life of Jesus*; he classed it with *Wally the Skeptic* as immoral, heretical, cynical, and antisocial, a serious threat to political order.[4] Ludwig von Gerlach (1795–1877), a Prussian government official, took time out from the festivities on Christmas Day in 1836 to send a plea to Ernst Wilhelm Hengstenberg (1802–69), an influential Berlin theologian, to use the widely read *Evangelical Church Newspaper* to expose the dangerous impact of *The Life of Jesus* not just on the church but on all German institutions.[5] And before long a group of Georg Wilhelm Friedrich Hegel's (1770–1831) disciples, among whom were Arnold Ruge (1802–80), Bruno Bauer (1809–82), Ludwig Feuerbach (1804–72), and, most notably, Karl Marx, made it a symbol of the radical political left.

Why did this academic book immediately cause panic-stricken terror in Germany? Why did liberal cultural critics, conservative government officials, and radical intellectuals alike find this study of the Bible a threat to social and political institutions? The answer is that *The Life of Jesus* implied a radical democratic politics similar to that espoused by Heine and by the young Marx. As it did in Leonard Krieger's *German Idea of Freedom*, the term *radical* in this book refers to groups in the 1830s "who were spurred on, far more than other liberal groups, by the consciousness of the abyss between theoretical idea and practical action and by the intensity of their striving to overcome it."[6] "Democrat," as Krieger said, had "no specific meaning until just before [1848]. . . . It tended to be appropriated by all those who believed in popular sovereignty as the theoretical basis and the ultimate culmination of the political process, but it included all varieties of analysis and proposals for the contemporary situation."[7] Accordingly, *democratic* will here refer not to a definite form of government but to a democratic principle held as an ideal by radicals who sought equality for all people in social and economic as well as political matters.

The politically liberal cultural critic Menzel, the government official von Gerlach, and the left-wing Hegelians are valuable historical guides to the explanation of the radical democratic politics of *The Life of Jesus*. Uncovering the sources for Menzel's association of the book with *Wally the Skeptic* leads us into German literary theory and to the politically concerned writers called the Young Germans. Uncovering the sources for von Gerlach's fears leads us into conservative politics and conservative Christianity in Prussia. Finally, uncovering the sources for the left-wing Hegelians' espousal of the work leads to the interrelations of Hegelian philosophy and political theory. The aspects of the German culture of the 1830s into which these readers of *The Life of Jesus* lead us provide a focus for examining those interconnections of political, social, economic, and intellectual elements that can make evident the idioms of that culture and thus the multiple signification of theological terms. The explanation of how *The Life of Jesus* caught up and changed those idioms to convey to Menzel, von Gerlach, and the left-wing Hegelians, among many others, a precise and radical political meaning, however, must begin with and continually readjust to a narrower focus: on the text itself, on its relation to the text of *Wally the Skeptic*, and on its use of the specialized language of the Hegelian philosophy.

The Life of Jesus: A Preliminary Description

Strauss presented *The Life of Jesus* as a scientific inquiry into "whether in fact, and to what extent, the ground on which we stand in the Gospels is historical."[8] He rejected for lack of evidence the assumption that the Gospels were eyewitness reports. Thus "every part" of the "whole history of Jesus" is considered open to critical examination, to the question of whether it is history or myth. Myth is defined as "the history-like forms of early Christian ideas which were formulated in sagas without conscious intention in the poetic process."[9]

According to Strauss, asking whether the gospel stories are history or myth could solve the faith problems of the nineteenth-century Christian. That Christian, heiress or heir "to the progress of mental cultivation," which is "the gradual recognition of a chain of causes and effects connecting natural phenomena with each other," sees discrepancies between truth as she or he knows it and what is recorded in the Gospels. In them, as in all sacred histories, "divine purposes seem to be immediately materialized," that is, to be effected without the mediation of the chain of causes and effects. Convinced of the truth of physical science, modern persons are "repulsed" by such narratives, and they think, "*The Divine cannot so have happened*; (not immediately, not in forms so rude;) or, *that which so happened cannot have been divine*."[10] In other words, accounts of miracles trouble moderns who understand the divine as working mediately, through the laws of nature. Thus if the Gospels, which tell of the divine working immediately in miracles, are to be meaningful, they must be interpreted.

Contemporary biblical interpretation failed to resolve doubts about the meaning of the Gospels because it insisted on affirming that the narratives were true history. The two predominant forms of this interpretation were the supernaturalist, which maintained, contrary to the justly perplexed believer, that the divine *did* immediately intervene in human history in the life of Jesus, and the rationalist, which maintained that the recorded miracles did happen but that there was a natural explanation for them left out by the scientifically unsophisticated gospel writers. Strauss contended that the supernaturalist interpreters abandoned science, while the rationalists gave up the divine, the content of religion. Only a mythical interpretation could be both scientific and true to the content of Christian faith. Such a view is at home with science because it does not defend a notion of the divine entering history immediately, and yet it is true to the content of Christian faith because it understands the gospel narratives as historylike forms of Christian ideas, *ideas* which are true.

To be both scientific and Christian was the stated goal of *The Life of Jesus*. Strauss attributed the feasibility of attaining this goal to the achievements of Hegelian philosophy. It influenced him to be freely critical by leading to an "internal liberation of the feelings and intellect from religious and dogmatical presuppositions,"[11] in part because it gave him assurance that "the essence of the Christian faith is perfectly independent of his criticism."[12] Thus as opposed to "the naturalist criticism of the [eighteenth century] which tried to subvert religious truth along with historical fact," *The Life of Jesus* set out to affirm that truth while openly questioning the fact status of the gospel narratives.[13]

The main body of the book is divided into two sections: a lengthy historical investigation and a brief Christian dogmatic conclusion. The object of the historical investigation was the gospel story of the life of Jesus. This aspect of *The Life of Jesus* needs to be emphasized. In general, modern biblical critics do not think that the Gospels are eyewitness reports, but they often seek the history of the gospel stories: that is, they ask Where and when did this story originate? How far back to Jesus' life can it be traced? In contrast, Strauss asked not about this history of the stories but simply whether the stories themselves were historical. He did so by first testing the plausibility of the supernaturalist and rationalist interpretations of them as historical. He asked whether they could be understood to be in agreement not only with the canons of physical science but also with a consistent chronology and a conceivable psychology of Jesus' life. Over and over again from the story of Jesus' birth to those of his getting lost in the temple, baptism, public preaching, miracles, passion, and death, he showed the supernaturalist and rationalist interpretations to be wanting and the mythical to be apt.

In the end, he judged many of the gospel narratives to be unconscious poetic products of the early Christian community, which formed them in creatively expressing its belief that Jesus was the Christ. In other words, "stimulated by the person and fate of Jesus, the early Christians shaped the picture of Christ having in mind unconsciously the idea of humanity in relation to Divinity."[14] This unconscious "idea of humanity in relation to Divinity" rooted several levels of myth formation. First and most concretely, it led the early Christians to reason that since Jesus was the Messiah, his life must have fulfilled the messianic promises of the Old Testament. Second, it led them to reason that such a life must have evidenced divine power, as did the miracle workers in their culture. Third, it led them to understand Jesus as fulfilling all divine purposes. The Christian thought that Jesus must have been born in Bethlehem as the prophets wrote, he must have worked miracles to manifest his divinity, and he must have been resurrected to demonstrate God's victory over sin and its punishment.

Strauss did locate some valid history of the man Jesus. What could be verified was that there was indeed a Jesus of Nazareth who preached an apocalyptic message of the Kingdom of God and who died a martyr's death. A real man did live whose actual life course was such that it could be associated with the dawning of the true idea of the relationship of the divine to the human. But Strauss denied that historical science could identify this human with the Christ figure delineated by Christian belief in the New Testament. The historical part of *The Life of Jesus* concluded that the Jesus of history was not the Christ of faith.

The second Christian dogmatic section of *The Life of Jesus* promised "to re-establish dogmatically that which has been destroyed critically."[15] That reestablishment entailed a second critical movement directed against the orthodox dogma of Christ. Strauss wrote:

> Hitherto our criticism had for its object the content of Christianity as historically presented in the gospel records; now this content having been called into question in its historical form assumes the form of a mental product and finds a refuge in the soul of the believer where it exists, not as a simple history but as a reflected history, that is, a confession of faith, a received dogma. Against this dogma appearing in its immediacy criticism *as a form of negativity and of the struggle for mediation* must certainly arise just as it must arise against any immediacy. Thus this criticism is no longer historical but rather dogmatic. It is only after faith has passed through both types of criticism that it is truly mediated or that it has become scientific knowledge.[16]

In this section Strauss described how from the time of their appearance the Gospels demanded interpretation and stated that in the Christological dogma the Church established the orthodox interpretation that Jesus was the Son of God, one person with two natures, fully divine and fully human, whose primary work was to die for the sins of humans. But then this dogma itself called for interpretation, and the struggle to appropriate the truth of Christology never ceased. As science itself developed, the struggle intensified until, with the appearance of the Hegelian philosophy in the nineteenth century, the tools were forged finally for a fully satisfying interpretation of the dogma of the God-man.

At the core of this eighteen-century-old struggle was the contradiction of declaring *one* person to be both human and divine. Hegelianism, rightly understood, provided the "key to the whole of Christology": "As the subject of the predicate which the Church assigns to Christ, we place, instead of an individual, an idea; but an idea which has an existence in reality, not in the mind only, like that of Kant. In an individual, a God-man, the properties and functions which the Church ascribes to Christ contradict themselves; in the idea of the human species they perfectly agree. Humanity is the union of the two natures—the incarnate God, the infinite Spirit alienated in the finite and the finite Spirit recollecting its infinitude."[17] Jesus of Nazareth is not the God-man; the truth of Christology is that the human species is the God-man.

Strauss gave a straightforward summary of the conclusion of *The Life of Jesus*: "Just as Plato's God formed the world by gazing at the Ideas, the early Christian community formed its image of Christ. Stimulated by the person and fate of Jesus, it shaped the picture of its Christ, having in mind unconsciously the idea of humanity in its relation to Divinity. The scientific knowledge of our time, however, can no longer repress the consciousness that the tie of the content of Christology to one individual belongs to a temporally and culturally conditioned form of this doctrine."[18]

Wally the Skeptic: A Preliminary Description

Wally the Skeptic is the story of a young German girl who belongs to the upper middle class. The novel is divided into three chronological books covering a little over a year in Wally's life. The first book is about the season of her innocent coquetry. It opens with the line "A white saddle horse being ridden at full gallop, a forest pierced by sunlight, Wally more beautiful than Aphrodite, imbued not only with every classical charm that might have arisen from Cypriot seas, but with all the magic of a romantic age and even the trappings of her own time, this last virtue seen less in her beauty itself than in the atmosphere surrounding it."[19] Wally rides her white horse past Caesar, a disillusioned but strong-charactered intellectual of her own class, who is walking alone in the woods, and she tosses five "costly" rings at his feet. After the two meet at a ball, Caesar duels with the five suitors who had given Wally the rings, and this courageous act initiates an intense flirtation. Caesar and Wally go with her aunt to a spa, where Wally becomes depressed. Caesar tries to brighten her mood with clever banter and stories about colorful locals, but both the banter and stories fail to lift Wally's spirits. In fact, the stories turn out to have real deaths as their endings. It is after they hear about one of the deaths that Wally and Caesar leave the spa.

The second book begins with a joyous Wally at a court ball telling Caesar that she is going to marry the Sardinian ambassador, Luigi. As her marriage day approaches Wally suffers "disquiet." She feels like "a living being placed in the vacuum glass of an air pump, or a bird who feels pain from within and without as air is extracted."[20] Although she yearns for Caesar, she goes ahead with her marriage.

Her transition from love "affairs" to marriage is marked by an idyllic scene in which on her wedding night she appears nude before Caesar as a pledge of her eternal love for him.[21] Wally moves to Paris and settles into her role as the wife of a nobleman with apparent ease, becoming nervous, reflective, and doubtful only about her religion, Christianity. But social conventions and the excitement of romantic idylls, as well as nineteenth-century Christianity, fail to give peace to Wally. Her husband uses her socially proper and unsuspecting habit of coquetry to bewitch his brother Jeronimo in order to gain control of the family fortune. The second book ends as, insane with unrequited love, Jeronimo commits suicide in front of Wally, who is thus awakened to Luigi's guile and flees from him. She turns back to Caesar, but he has made plans to marry Delphine, a Jewish woman to whom he is attracted because she is free from both the class and religious proscriptions that plague Wally.

The first part of the third book relates Wally's reflections on her specific plight, on being a woman in her society, and on religion. She turns back to Caesar one more time, this time to give her religious solace. In response he sends her a biting attack on the New Testament and the dogma of Christ. This attack takes away the "mainstay" of Wally's life. Gutzkow asks of her, "She, the skeptic, the uncertain one, the foe of God, was she not more pious than those who reassure themselves with a misunderstood faith?"[22] Finally, shortly after receiving Caesar's theological letter, Wally stabs herself to death. "She lay there, not smiling and peaceful as may be true in other cases, but rather with her lovely face cramped in distortion and an expression of despair in the staring eyes that was terrifying."[23]

Under the censorship decree, issued 19 December 1835, the few remaining copies of *Wally the Skeptic* were confiscated from bookstores and discussion of the novel was prohibited in most regions of Germany. Furthermore, the Federal government censored the work of Gutzkow's supposed literary colleagues, Ludolf Wienbarg (1802–72), Theodor Mundt (1808–61), Heinrich Laube (1806–84), and Heinrich Heine. This literary group was named Young Germany, and those in the group who had not already fled Germany, as had Heine, served prison terms. Strauss had no contacts with the members of this group, and he had not read the story of Wally when he wrote his theology book addressed to modern doubt.[24] On his part, Gutzkow did not design Wally's doubt from that described in, or provoked by, *The Life of Jesus*.[25] Yet the stability of German cultural ideals was almost simultaneously and equally threatened by the story of a German Aphrodite who reveals herself to be a nervous, self-destructive coquette and a scientific historical examination of the gospel narratives which reveals itself as the true meaning of Hegelianism.

The Language of Hegelianism

The theological and political meanings of Hegel's philosophy are embedded in the entirety of his philosophical project, which is nothing less than the project of attaining absolute truth. In execution this project takes the form of a journey through a dimly lit labyrinth full of a myriad of shapes from all ages of history and all realms of human culture. For Hegel, the truth and the whole were synonymous. The whole encompassed the entire rich content of human history and experience; it was not simply a universal reducible to laws or structures. Nevertheless, the attainment of absolute truth was not a gathering together of all the aspects of history and experience. It entailed a recreation of the way humans know their content-rich world; this recreation called for a new logic and thus a new language. Therefore, the Hegelian philosophy speaks a specialized language which asserts a total comprehensiveness. In effect, this philosophy defines a world of its own that it claims to be the real world.

It is important to recognize this aspect of the Hegelian philosophy because it can explain how the Hegelians of the 1830s could use its language as though it were everyday language and draw direct implications for governmental policy from complex philosophical discussions of the nature of Absolute Spirit or true subjectivity. To see these implications, however, it is essential to stay free of the philosophical labyrinth that traps many historians of ideas. Yet a familiarity with some Hegelian words and with some aspects of the Hegelian logic is necessary in tracing the links between this specialized language and the general idioms of the culture.[26]

For the purposes of this study the way to enter the Hegelian system while retaining a safe exit will be to concentrate on the Hegelian terms for God and Christ as they bear on three interrelated questions that are at the root of the politically significant linkage points between the languages at issue here: Is Hegel's God the personal God of the orthodox, biblical Christian tradition? Is Hegel's Christ the God-man of that tradition? How do Hegel's concepts of God and Christ relate to the concept of sovereignty?

Hegel developed his philosophical language, and thus his terms for God and Christ, out of the heritage of German Idealism and Romanticism. The two figures representing these trends who are most important for our understanding of God and Christ in the Hegelian philosophy are Immanuel Kant (1724–1804) and Friedrich Schleiermacher (1768–1834). Central to German Idealism was the awareness of the "I," of the knowing subject as somehow separating itself from everything objective in the world and making itself into an object to itself. Here the focus is on the "I" as the necessary and prior condition of all knowing. In this sense it was what Hegel called the abstract universal. The "I" could also carry with it the connotation of free individuality or a definite self distinct from or exclusive of all determination by anything or anyone else. This "I" Hegel called the abstract individual. Central to German Romanticism, in the version important here, is the sense of the desire for unity of the "I" with the rich, differentiated world of objects and persons outside of it. This unity was to be achieved in an immediate and often intuitive way.

It was Kant who set the stage for the post-Enlightenment crises and defenses of Christian faith in Germany. Enlightenment reason in general had left little room for a personal God or for his Son, Jesus Christ, as the God-man of traditional Christian faith. A reason capable of attaining truth on its own needed no biblical revelation of truth conveyed through supernatural acts of the personal God and his Son. God lived, of course, but as the first premise of the natural laws in the world, which human reason was designed to comprehend autonomously.

In his *Critique of Pure Reason* (1781), Kant directly challenged this Enlightenment God by challenging the truth of metaphysical knowledge. He denied that any knowledge of *supersensible* reality could be attained, whether that knowledge was of what things are in themselves, as opposed to how they appear to the senses, or was theological knowledge of God. In other words, he maintained that metaphysical speculation (*Vernunft*) could not come to know a transcendent natural law or its ground, a rational God, by way of knowledge of the sensible world. To extend the categories by which one knows the sensible world, the categories of the understanding (*Verstand*), beyond the finite as sensibly experienced is invalid. Those categories cannot be traced to what things really are in themselves out there in the world; they are innate categories of the human mind. In short, Kant denied that reason could attain absolute truth and thus knowledge of the Enlightenment God. Moreover, the *Critique of Pure Reason* left little room for the personal God of biblical tradition to reappear in the void that it created because it declared irrational any conjunction of an absolute with finite and sensible qualities.

In his later works, Kant admitted the importance to humans of an idea of absolute perfection and the rationality of assuming that this idea exists in order for human morality to be fulfilled and for the mandate of conscience not to be in vain. Kant found this idea in practical not scientific reason, and he called its reality a "postulate," an assumption or matter of faith. He argued that the moral law—to act according to universal principles rather than selfish, individualistic ones and thus to treat all humans, even oneself, as ends and not as means—is a universal fact of moral reason. The goal of this moral law is the community of free individuals. The attainment of the goal of the moral law is guaranteed by the reality of freedom, of God, and of immortality. But the knowledge of such metaphysical realities as these is, by Kant's definition, beyond the reach of scientific reason. Kant deduced, nevertheless, that if humans are indeed morally obligated to attain the goal of the moral law, freedom *must be* real and there *must be* a God and immortality to ensure that humans can attain the goal of moral actions and the rewards for them that they do not receive on earth. Thus the assumption of the truth of freedom, God, and immortality is rationally justified.

Kant correlated the ideal of the moral perfection of humanity, the harmonious community of free individuals, with the idea of a human archetype. This archetype is called a son of God because he is a perfect person willing to die for the good of others. Kant found in the Christian scriptures a picture of this archetype in the story of Jesus Christ, but he denied that it was rational to assume that one specific person in history could be or truly was this son of God.

Schleiermacher kept some of Kant's distinction between realms of truth, defining religion as "feeling," an aspect of human consciousness distinct from, but not in conflict with, autonomous scientific reason. Religion is thus a feeling of absolute dependence on God, a consciousness of God that informs, but is not identical with, theoretical reason or morality. Schleiermacher attempted to show how a religious archetype, in contrast to Kant's archetype as the rational ideal of perfection, could be actual in Jesus Christ in history. He used suggestions of the category of genius to describe this Jesus as one who through his own unique and perfect God-consciousness introduced into history the human potential of religious perfection. Jesus' "feeling," his God-consciousness constituting his genius, was an immediate, scientifically inexplicable relation between his human self-consciousness and the source of all existence, God.[27]

Hegel's most famous declaration against Kant was also applicable to Schleiermacher and the movement of Romanticism that he helped found. Hegel wrote that "what is rational is actual."[28] Exactly what this declaration meant philosophically, politically, and theologically was at the heart of the Hegelian debates in the 1830s. To Hegel's theological students, it seemed to create, in contrast to Schleiermacher, the scientifically explicable conditions for demonstrating that Kant's rational archetype of Christ was actual, that is, historical.

Hegel himself directly acknowledged the problem of a modern, post-Enlightenment comprehension of a Christ designated as the God-man. It was, he said, a contradiction for the understanding, and comprehending it was the most difficult aspect of trying philosophically to deal with religion. He placed the doctrine of the Incarnation at the center of Christianity, however, and he declared that Christianity was the absolute, the most perfect, religion. Moreover, he claimed repeatedly that his philosophy had the same content as the Christian religion and that it thus differed from Christianity only in form. The form in religion is the representation (*Vorstellung*), a thought which has a sensuous component like the images present in the mind at the level of perception of the outside world. Philosophy, by contrast, has the form of the concept (*Begriff*), of universal thought, of the logic of reality itself.

In short, there is no doubt that Hegel claimed that his philosophy could logically comprehend that contradiction presented to ordinary reason by the Christian doctrine of the God-man. Indeed, the central claim of his philosophy is to comprehend contradiction, to logically think contradiction as necessarily constitutive of the truth and not merely as an abstract rule for judging an incorrect use of principles.

Therefore, with the sun of the Enlightenment still casting some light on German soil, Hegel promised to revive the orthodox doctrine of the God-man and place it at the center of a scientific, comprehensive, and fully articulated philosophy. To keep this promise he created the labyrinth. In other words, his claim to comprehend the central Christian doctrine of the Incarnation was dependent on his demonstration that knowledge of the absolute was attainable.

Hegel agreed with Kant that the understanding (*Verstand*), common rationalism, with its categories of ordinary empirical science, cannot attain knowledge of the absolute, but against Kant he held that true metaphysical reason (*Vernunft*) is capable of reaching such truth. Whereas the understanding functions to make clear and exact the differences between finite objects, another level of thought, named simply *reason*, comprehends finite things as they are in themselves as well as the infinite and its unity with the finite. Reason thus comprehends contradiction, sees beyond what at first appears to be the mutual exclusion of the finite and infinite to the truth that the infinite and the finite are necessarily and mutually interrelated. Thus to know the finite world fully and adequately and to attain knowledge of the absolute are one and the same. In Hegelian language the absolute truth is named *Absolute Spirit* and, often, simply God. Absolute Spirit can be defined in a preliminary way as the process of infinite idea becoming actual in the alien realm of finite nature and yet thereby developing self-recognition. In this development it moves to negate the finite, which is always marked by particularity and singleness, and yet in some way also to preserve it. Put in Hegel's language Absolute Spirit sublates (from the German *aufheben*) its otherness in the finite. It is important to keep in mind that sublation is not a simple negation of the finite. This does not imply, however, that Absolute Spirit is merely an unending series of preserved finite individuals. Such an absolute Hegel called *Bad Infinity*.

At the root of Hegel's treatment of the meaning of Absolute Spirit, and thus God, are basic philosophical questions about the relation of thought and being: How are the knowing subject and the objective physical world interrelated? How can subjectivity and objectivity be understood as unified? Hegel believed that the entire history of philosophy, and, in a way, all of previous history, contributed to the discovering of the true answer to these questions. In his own day philosophy, while not reaching the truth, had attained a pregnant formulation of the question. German Idealist and Romantic philosophers had redefined the pole of thought or subject as the pole of self-consciousness, and the pole of being or substance as the intuited, yet inarticulated, sense of the unity of essence and existence. In Hegel's own words, the attainment of absolute truth, the knowledge of Absolute Spirit, depended on comprehending and articulating the true as equally substance and subject. The problem of the unity of substance and subject was to be solved as the problem of the unity of the intrinsic identity (Kant's in-itself) of what exists with self-consciousness.

Hegel aligned himself at the start of his search for truth on the side of his predecessors who tried to grasp directly the unity of thought and being rather than on the side of Kant, who began with a reflection on the pole of thought and the conditions of knowledge. Hegel identified the goal of his own project with the goal of Spinoza's (1632–77) philosophy of substance, and he recognized this to be the goal of the early Schelling (1775–1854), as well as of Schleiermacher and the other members of the school of German Romanticism. But all of these philosophers had failed to attain the truth of the unity of thought and being, in Hegel's opinion, because they had not been able adequately to deal with the contradictions posed by common rationalism. They could only understand God as the *all* of being, not as the "I" of a subject who is self-defining. They understood God either as an all into which everything individual disappeared or as the all that sounds a single note when each individual is grasped. Their concept of God was pantheist. They had, Hegel said, "too much God," and thus lost a differentiated, finite world.

Kant, at the other extreme, despite his recognition of the role of the subject, the "I," in knowing, had "too little God," a rationalist God. Kant separated God as an idea of practical reason, as a mere ought to be, from theoretical knowledge of the actual; this separation of knowledge of the infinite from knowledge of the finite amounted, in Hegel's analysis, to representing God as permanently and irretrievably beyond the finite. God may be a subject "up there," but this God has no real world belonging to "him." This God then is no bigger than a finite individual "I" would be without any relation to something outside the self. It is merely an unrelated, exclusive unit —a little isolated "I," a very little God indeed, far smaller than the personal Christian God or the God of the Enlightenment.

Hegel declared that the truth of the unity of thought and being could not be attained by the simple negations that were exercised in one form or another by the pantheist or rationalist systems of his predecessors. They could only hold on to *one* pole (the reality of the universal, the All, or the reality of the individual, the single and determined), while negating the other. They failed to exercise the *duplex negatio affirmat*, the double negation of true reason which results in the preservation of both poles, subject and substance, the universal and the individual, thought and being, in effect, God and the world full of differentiated objects.

Hegel wrote that his system only differed from a philosophy of being, which was most notably represented by Spinoza in more modern times, by its recognition of the concept of individuality that was introduced to the world by Christianity. Here again is his claim that his philosophy comprehends the central Christian doctrine of the Incarnation: God become a finite human individual. In this case, however, he asserts that this Incarnation in some way makes possible his philosophy and, thus, absolute knowing.

How the Christian doctrine of the Incarnation makes possible, or, rather, is a necessary presupposition of, the Hegelian philosophy of Absolute Spirit is the issue raised by *The Life of Jesus*. Hegel asserted that in Christ as the God-man the world received the truth of Absolute Spirit, although in an implicit, not fully articulated form. In the God-man, the true mode of union between thought and being, the universal and the individual, subject and substance, God and the world was made evident to the human knower. What the knower sees in the God-man is what mediates between these poles without destroying them; it sees an individual self-consciousness. This means that because God in Christ unites with the finite and does not destroy it, Christianity introduced to the world a concept of a universal which preserves and does not destroy the individual. The logic utilized by common rationalism cannot grasp this sort of universal. It works with the rigid categories of universal, particular, and individual, and it cannot unite necessarily the individual and the universal. But true reason, as informed by Christianity's contribution to history in the God-man, who is the true form of the necessary unity of the universal and the individual, recognizes that true individuality is identical with true universality. True individuality is not a one-way retreat from the universal. In other words, the individual as something clearly particular, unique, exclusive, and single—that is, as finite—is not the simple opposite of the universal. In Christ, true individuality shows itself to be identical with true subjectivity. Since true subjectivity is *self-consciousness*, it is also universal in the sense of that "I" of German Idealism which is the necessary and prior condition of all knowing and thus is a unity or a whole distinguishable from all particularity. This is the "I" which Hegel named the abstract universal. In Christ this was united with what he called the abstract individual, that "I" which is unique, self-determining, and exclusive. In Christ the abstract universal and the abstract individual form the concrete universal. The middle term, binding these forms of universal and individual together and providing them their identity, is the true "I," or self-consciousness.

Obviously, only a new logic with new terms to replace universal, particular, and individual could promise to make any sense out of these assertions. The terms of Hegel's new logic are *Idea*, *Spirit*, and *Nature*, which, in contrast to the terms of ordinary logic, are fluid and necessarily flow or turn into one another in a living process. What ultimately is brought forth in Hegel's system as making sense of or comprehending his assertions about the Incarnation is the philosophical explication, the scientific logic, of Absolute Spirit. Philosophy recognizes Absolute Spirit as the subjectivity of substance, that is, as self-consciousness generating through idea the world of nature as a necessary moment in its own process of development as self-consciousness. In recognizing this, philosophy must realize that finite self-consciousness is the locus of Spirit's return out of its own self-alienation in nature and thus in the form of self-consciousness the finite itself is a necessary moment of Spirit's own self-recognition. In its true essence, Absolute Spirit is self-conscious life.

Thus Hegel's philosophy adopted a model of life for truth in place of the Enlightenment's mechanistic or mathematical model. In contrast to the mathematical model, which reduces everything to general and abstract laws, on the one hand, and individual units, on the other, and thus keeps the individual and universal separate, the model of life, which is a model of the whole as an organism, promised to account for an inner purposiveness that held individuals together without destroying uniqueness and independence. In such a model the universal becomes, in a sense, a whole, with its own individuality to which specific elements, which retain their own individuality, are essentially united and are thus themselves universal.

There is a basic ambiguity about the model of life itself, however. Karl Mannheim explained: "[In one form] as a mode of thought [the model of life] conceives the world as thoroughly alive, but it assumes that one can find in it hidden sequences and analogues. [This] tendency to think in analogies is still not wholly opposed to the ordinary method of thought which looks for generally valid laws in the world since—in its own curious way—this form of thought, too, endeavors to find general laws—that is, morphological laws of succession."[29] In other words, a common rationalism *could* in some sense find itself at home with this form of the model of life. In another form, however, life could provide a model of uniqueness which "abandons even the analogy as a pattern of regularity"—every moment and every thing is seen as unique.[30] In the first form ordinary thought has some degree of legitimate and innate capacity to discover general patterns of the world and even of history. In the second it seems ordinary thought is always subordinate to the evidence of life, to what is given to it. In other words, while the model of life can resolve the issue of the universal and the individual on one level, it presents it again as the issue of logic and history. How is history, if it is defined as the recognition of the uniqueness of every moment of life, related to logic, which by definition claims the generality of science?

Hegel did criticize certain types of philosophies of life that he thought collapsed back into the same emptiness as common rationalism. Specifically, he attacked the intuitive system of the early Schelling on this account, and by using a model of life as self-consciousness rather than as biology, he sought to avoid "the night in which all cows are black" into which he claimed that Schelling's philosophy took one.[31] Thus a social model —that is, interpersonal communication—provides Hegel the mode of uniting the individual and the universal. In other words, it is the interplay *between* self-consciousnesses that binds the universal and the individual. This interplay, named spirit, is constituted by a moral unity or whole, and it is somewhat analogous to the ethos of a group. Ultimately, Hegel identifies purpose or will as the truth of the whole. But this purpose does not have the form of abstract law or the form of exclusive individuality. It has the form of spirit, mutually interrelated individuality.

Does this social model of life solve the problem of the relation of history and logic? Hegel claimed that philosophy is the comprehension of the content of the Christian religion, which is a positive, historical religion, and that philosophy merely makes explicit in a scientific logic what is present only implicitly, in representational form, in it. Is philosophy thus dependent on, subordinate to, what is given in history? If so, does it eliminate all vestiges of the principles of analogy found also in common rationalism and ordinary science? Does it assert that the actual, in the sense of the historical uniqueness of every moment, is the rational? Does it assert that what claims factual status, either in the past or in the present, is rational? Or, on the other hand, does Hegel's logic retain some relation to ordinary logic and thus transcend the uniqueness of what is handed to it by life and history in some sort of generality? Put theologically, this line of questioning becomes the query: Is Hegel's logic of the Incarnation a defense of its factual historical status?

Hegel said that his logic describes the essence of God, of God as self-consciousness and thus as the interrelations of the Trinity, as it was before the creation. In other words, the eternal interplay of self-consciousnesses is the basic model for the unity of subject and substance, the universal and the individual. But in what sort of shape does self-consciousness achieve this unity after the creation or in history? Is it the self-consciousness of the personal, albeit trinitarian, God of the orthodox biblical tradition, who, acting like an individual, freely achieves "his" purposes in history? Is it the self-consciousness of the unique individual Jesus Christ, the God-man of the Christian tradition, who truly existed as a fact of human history? Is it the self-consciousness of a specific group of people, for example, a nation? Or, rather, is it the general, collective human self-consciousness as it develops in history?

In political form, the question of whose self-consciousness provides the unity of universal and individual becomes a question about sovereignty. What type of sovereignty, monarchial or popular, can provide the unity of human collectivity? The theological and the political form of the question meet as the question: What type of sovereignty corresponds to Hegel's concept of God and Christ?

Politics and the Idea of Christ

In the 1830s, just as, for example, at the times of Chalcedon and the Reformation, politics and the subtleties of the theological attempts to define the object of Christian faith, Jesus Christ, were intertwined. In short, definitions of Christ carried political as well as theological meanings. Hegelian theology in particular demonstrated this because the dicta grounding a Christology were taken from Hegel's *Philosophy of Right*. Many of his students found a direct justification for the historical existence of Christ in the statement made in reference to the legitimacy of monarchy—"All historical actions, including world-historical actions, culminate with individuals as subjects giving actuality to the substantial."[32] Indeed, Marx was to judge that it had been Hegel's intent in his *Philosophy of Right* to represent the "monarch as the actual 'God-man,' as the actual Incarnation of the Idea."[33]

Several years before Marx associated Hegelian theology and monarchist politics, David Friedrich Strauss, in discussing the response to *The Life of Jesus* by theological Hegelians, applied political terms to their positions. In question was Hegel's assertion that "what is rational is actual," and Strauss gave names from the political positions in the French parliament to the different ways in which this dictum was interpreted by theological Hegelians. The theologians on the Hegelian "right" used the dictum to ground the assertion that the existence of a God-man is rational and thus that the historical validity (actuality) of all the gospel narratives about Jesus Christ could be rationally deduced from the Idea. The theologians of the Hegelian "center" used it to ground the assertion that the historical validity of *some* of the gospel narratives could be deduced. Strauss put himself alone on the Hegelian "left," where he held that only scientific historical investigation could prove the historical validity of the gospel narratives: the rationality of the Idea of the God-man could not validate any history that was not tested.[34]

The designations *right* and *left* in the French parliament stemmed from the political stances assumed in the Revolution of 1789, more commonly named "aristocratic" and "democratic." In Germany, especially, the French Revolution was understood as a fight between "aristocracy" and "democracy," and as will be seen in the next chapter, those terms, rather than the more neutral ones "right" and "left," were part of Germany's own quite different struggle with the question of freedom. If the political right is defined as it was generally in that age as espousing the conservation of a divinely validated political past and the left as that which considers any political arrangement valid only when tested by a set of criteria derived from common human assent, then the naming of the theological position of the Hegelians who would conserve the entirety of the gospel narratives as history as "right" and Strauss's position as "left" was apt. In this instance, however, Strauss's naming of Hegelian schools would turn out to be more than a clever play with words. *The Life of Jesus* did in fact split right from left in Germany; the book made actual its author's analogy.

In 1839, Arnold Ruge would use the terms *democracy* and *aristocracy* to describe the different conclusions of two different editions of Strauss's *Life of Jesus*. He named the Christ presented at the end of the third edition, which appeared in 1838, aristocratic, and he contrasted this figure to the Christ of the 1835 edition, which he named democratic.

In referring to the Germans' quest for political freedom, Marx wrote, "In politics, the Germans have thought what the other nations have done."[35] In other words, while other nations, most notably France, were changing their governmental structures in the direction of increased freedom and participation, Germany, despite, as will be seen, the disparate changes caused by Napoleon's invasion, remained the same. Persons in Germany heard about the struggles for freedom, the battles between aristocracy and democracy in other countries, and they thought about them. Indeed they generated a system of thought about freedom of thought—Idealism. Marx maintained that the principles of the French Revolution had influenced Germany in its philosophy, but they had not changed actual conditions.

Heine agreed and described how the principles of revolution entered German thought:

> Lessing died in Brunswick in 1781, misunderstood, hated and denounced. In the same year Immanuel Kant's *Critique of Pure Reason* appeared in Königsberg. With this book, which due to a strange delay did not become known until the end of the decade, there began in Germany an intellectual revolution which presents the most striking analogies to the material revolution in France and which seems to more profound thinkers just as important. . . . On both sides of the Rhine we see the same break with the past; as in France every privilege must be justified, so, in Germany, must every thought be justified, and just as here the monarchy, the keystone of the old social order, so there [theism], the keystone of the old intellectual regime, has fallen.[36]

Heine equated Kant's *Critique of Pure Reason*, which he named theism's 21st of January, with the beheading of Louis XVI in 1793. Moreover, this was the day, he said, on which the personal God of biblical tradition, the God of Germany's past, was eliminated for German thought, and he asked: "Do you hear the little [hand] bell ringing? Kneel down. They are bringing the sacraments to a dying god."[37]

God did not die for German thought or politics. By the 1830s, Hegel and Schleiermacher had promised to demonstrate how religion and modern thought could be reconciled. But in 1835, Strauss's *Life of Jesus* appeared, and it reintroduced revolutionary principles into German thought with as much force as Kant's *Critique* had done a generation earlier.

Chapter Two ✣ Germany in the 1830s ✣ Politics, Literature, and Religion

In 1830, in the tiny southwest German village of Klein-Ingersheim, high on a bluff overlooking the Neckar River in Würtemberg, recent Tübingen graduate David Friedrich Strauss faced his first congregation. It was made up of small farmers, and on this Sunday they had just lost their crop of grapes in a storm. Such a loss was not uncommon, since the grape is an unstable crop, but unless the growers had savings to cover such an off year, the loss could mean starvation. In this part of Germany the majority of farmers owned their lands, but they were subject to a law stipulating that family lands were to be divided among the children. Thus, the family plots grew progressively smaller, jeopardizing not only the farmers' ability to accumulate reserves but also their year-to-year subsistence.[1] Confronted with this crisis in his congregation, the youth Strauss preached: "Yes my friends, better to perish from lack of earthly bread than suffer from a lack of heavenly manna, the word of God! Better to go without the fruit of our vineyards than the spiritual drink from the Rock which is Christ! And so it has happened to you! The Lord has struck your fields, but not so that you must hunger; and he has preserved for you his word and his church."[2]

Several years later in another southwest German village, Butzbach, in nearby Hesse-Darmstadt, an experienced pastor, Friedrich Ludwig Weidig (1791–1837), sent the following words in the *Hessian Courier* to another group of small farmers:

FREEDOM FOR THE HUTS!
WAR ON THE PALACES!

. . . The life of the farmer is a long workday. Strangers devour his fields before his very eyes, his body is a callus, his sweat the salt on the aristocrats' table. . . . You are paying 6,000,000 guilders to a handful of persons in the Grand Duchy to whose capricious attitudes your lives and property are entrusted, and it is the same for all others in our dismembered Germany. You *are* nothing. You *have* nothing! . . . Indeed they may threaten you with implements and mounted soldiers of kings, but I say to you: Whosoever raises a sword against the people, he shall also perish by the people's sword. Germany is now a field of battle, soon it will be a paradise. The German people is a *single* body, you are a member of it. It is immaterial where this seeming corpse begins to move and show signs of life. When the Lord gives you His sign through the men through whom he will lead the people from servitude into freedom, then raise yourselves up and the whole body will rise up with you.[3]

These two Christian exhortations urged dramatically different responses to the economic hardships of the German peasantry. The first counseled acceptance of such hardships, which were said to pall before spiritual rewards. The hardship was seen as an "act of God." But the ability of the farmer to survive the blows of unfavorable weather conditions was related to the overall conditions of agricultural life, a fact which Strauss's sermon ignored. Thus, if only by omission, it supported the prevailing order of the peasant village. Weidig's exhortation, on the other hand, insisted on recognition of the social conditions and called upon the poor and suffering "body" of the Lord to revolt against the prevailing order.

During the years from 1830 to 1848 the hardships of groups in villages and towns throughout Germany intensified, and, finally, violent revolution broke out. This revolution did not represent a victory for the liberating political logic of the Word of God preached by Weidig, however, and it did not transform Germany from "a field of battle" into the Lord's "paradise" that he had desired. In fact, as Theodore Bigler has stated, German Protestantism failed "to side with the people during [and] after the Revolution of 1848." In his opinion this failure "had the painful consequence of alienating the German masses from the Church and eventually driving them to embrace the secular religions of Marxism and National Socialism."[4]

The work of the young Klein-Ingersheim pastor is an essential part of this story of the interrelationship of Protestant Christianity and politics in nineteenth-century Germany. Strauss's 1830 sermon is, of course, an element of the story; it typifies the ecclesiastical wisdom offered to the emerging German masses. But the 1835 edition of Strauss's *Life of Jesus*, his work of academic biblical criticism, is a major character in the history of pre-1848 Germany. In fact, this criticism of the Word of God had more importance in determining the course of revolutionary ferment than did pronouncements of the Word's wordly eschatological meaning.

Throughout Germany, in state bureaucracies, coffeehouses, and beer halls, as well as in church pulpits and basements, *The Life of Jesus* would be discussed not as a technical academic treatise but as a political symbol—or rather as divergent political symbols of sedition against the state, on the one hand, and political free choice, on the other. The most significant aspect of the age bearing on its political meaning was the union of throne and altar. The prominent conservative political philosopher Julius Stahl (1802–61) said that in the revolution of 1848 there were only two sides—"one for the revolution and the other for the throne and altar."[5] Churches were branches of government, and to the extent that "the half-feudal political structure of Germany was brought into question" by those desiring change so were the state churches "so closely associated with it."[6] On the "right" men of authority in these churches stood together with the kings, so the "left" inevitably criticized the behavior of official Christianity. In Prussia, the largest and most important German Protestant state, church administration was an especially tightly controlled department of the central state administration, and thus Christianity in Prussia was most often the reference of the "left" for its discussion of religion. With this in mind, Heine's words should be heard again.

It is important at the moment to neutralize the power of religion. You see, we Germans are in the same situation as you were before the revolution, when Christianity and the old regime formed an absolutely inseparable alliance. This could not be destroyed as long as Christianity still exerted its influence on the masses. Voltaire had to start up his cutting laughter before Samson [the executioner in Paris during the French Revolution] could let his axe fall.[7]

With *The Life of Jesus*, Strauss became Germany's Voltaire. Yet as Heine himself saw, despite the similarity between the prerevolutionary French alliance of the Christian church and state and that in Germany in the 1830s, religion in Protestant Germany, in Luther's Germany, carried a meaning not found in France. Inevitably, the criticism of religion would have a different shape and produce different political results.

Restoration and Pre-March

The unsettled political conditions in early nineteenth-century Germany are reflected in the two designations commonly given to the years between the expulsion of Napoleon's troops in 1813 and the revolution of 1848. One name is *Restauration* (Restoration), a term first made famous in the work of Karl Ludwig von Haller (1768–1854), who advocated that the states of central Europe return the rights of their monarchs and aristocracy to their pre-Napoleonic status, thereby abolishing the legal reforms of a basically feudal order brought about during French occupation.[8] The other name given to the years 1815–48 is *Vormärz* (Pre-March), referring to the momentum leading to the 1848 revolution. Prominent on this side of early-nineteenth-century German history were the many voices that, in diverse, even disparate ways, sought an extension of the social and political rights brought to commoners by Napoleon's invasion. Paradoxically, the inclusion of these commoners in German armies formerly reserved for aristocrats, which created the military force necessary to expel Napoleon, planted in the people a sense of their right to participate in government, as well as the desire to have a united Germany on the model of other European nation states.

The formal political organization of Germany from 1815 to 1848, the German Confederation, which was established at the Congress of Vienna in 1815, was headed by Austria, Germany's leading Catholic power. It did not constitute Germany as a united nation, nor did it foster broad-based representative government. This confederation met in assembly at Frankfurt. Representation was by aristocrats appointed by the kings of its thirty-nine states, and its policies, which were controlled by Metternich (1773–1859), the chancellor of Austria, consistently favored restoration.

Hopes for national unity and representative government did not totally die out after the Congress of Vienna, however. Imbued with the military spirit of the Wars of Liberation, student associations served as the principle vehicles for keeping them alive. In October 1817 at the Wartburg these *Burschenschaften* celebrated Napoleon's defeat and Martin Luther's proclamation of his theses; they burned copies of Von Haller's books on restoration in the name of a German freedom and identity rooted in the Reformation, which for them symbolized freedom from the repressive action of Metternich of Catholic Austria. Two years after Wartburg a member of one of the *Burschenschaften*, a theology student, Karl Sand (1795–1820), murdered Alexander Kotzebue (1761–1819), a poet who vigorously supported the Restoration. In reaction the Federal Diet approved a set of decrees put forth by Metternich to outlaw the *Burschenschaften* and to establish press censorship and inspectors for the universities. Throughout the 1820s these so-called Carlsbad decrees were the charter for a generally successful repression of opposition to the Restoration.

In these circumstances, as would be expected, there was no organization of those desiring the furtherance of the rights of commoners and their representation in a shadow government parallel to the Diet of the Confederation. The edicts of the Frankfurt Diet prohibited such political assembly. Thus the galvanizing of those desiring a more representative government had to overcome the powerful restraints of the dominant Restoration forces, and it had to be expressed in cultural forms other than the overtly political. Paramount among those in the 1830s was religion, or, more aptly, Christian theology. In 1843, Ludwig Feuerbach wrote to Arnold Ruge that "theology is for

Germany the only practical and successful vehicle for politics, at any rate for the moment."[9]

In the fourth decade of the nineteenth century internal economic changes and foreign political events, along with new religious thought, began to cast a shadow over the goal of the Restoration. Theodore Hamerow has pointed out that what the restored dynasties were "trying to impose from above by legislation, the silent forces of economic development were undermining from below."[10] This subversive force for economic development was the emergence of the middle class, which was facilitated by two events in mid-decade: the formation in 1834 of the Customs Union to remove tariff barriers between most of the German states and the opening of the first section of railroad line in 1835. These innovations were to bring about an economic and intellectual union that preceded any political union between the individual German states.

The political event that unsettled German peace was the French revolution in Paris in July of 1830. In the year that Strauss was graduating from his theological studies at Tübingen and moving to Klein-Ingersheim as pastor, the French deposed Charles X in a popular uprising. They placed Louis Philippe on the throne as lieutenant general of the Kingdom of France and liberalized the constitution, the Charte of 1814. This revolution reawakened the hopes in Germany for representative government and the emerging middle class brought pressure in many states for the granting of constitutions. In 1832 proponents of democracy gathered at Hamburg in a festival reminiscent of Wartburg, and in 1833 a group of radicals made an unsuccessful putsch against the Federal Diet. Although not involved in the actual attack, Weidig had been a participant in the initial planning for a takeover of this body. The following year he and the coauthor of the *Hessian Courier*, Georg Büchner (1813–37), held secret meetings on revolutionary tactics with peasants in Badenburg.

The powers of the Restoration reacted to this ferment by intensifying the censorship of the press and of universities, by limiting local assemblies, and by attempting to stop the move on the part of a few individual states to grant limited constitutions. By 1834 calm seemed to have returned. In the *Hessian Courier*, Weidig and Büchner reported:

In Germany, however, and in the remainder of Europe, there was great rejoicing when Charles X was deposed, and the suppressed German states armed themselves in the battle for freedom. The princes deliberated together on how to escape the fury of the people, and the crafty among them said: "Let us hand over a part of our authority so that we may keep the rest." And they appeared before the people and said: "We want to present you with the very freedom for which you are about to fight." And trembling with fear they threw down a few scraps and spoke of their mercy. Unfortunately the people trusted them and went to sleep.[11]

Sleep and *The Epigonen*: The Contrasts of Culture

Sleep was a favorite metaphor of German poets during this period, and they used it in both praise and criticism of the culture. Although literary historians disagree on what name to give to the period, the most common term is *Biedermeier*, which connotes a beautiful and content society, characterized by happy families, untroubled by social and political change. One of Strauss's biographers places his early education in such a *Biedermeier* setting: "At the foot of the Swabian Alb, a few miles northwest of Ulm, where the placid waters of the Blau river—a leisurely flowing stream—wind their way toward the Danube, the gently sloping Blau Valley begins to rise to a small plateau at its head. Here nestles the sleepy little town of Blaubeuren, surrounded by a semi-circle of steep, thickly wooded hillside."[12] Lists of the best *Biedermeier* writers include Edward Möricke (1804–75), Strauss's friend and fellow theologian. In 1847, the year before the revolution, Möricke wrote the following poem:

IN THE PARK

Look, the chestnut tree's are still children,
they hang here as moist as the
Wing of the butterfly when it has just left its wrap;
But a short rain in a gentle night brings to unfolding
Softly the fanshaped leaves. Quickly they cover the path.
—You may hurry, O heavenly spring, or you may linger,
Always a wonder, you flee past our enraptured eye.[13]

Along with its interest in apparently unimportant things such as chestnut leaves, *Biedermeier* literature is considered supportive of contentment "with a very modest share in life."[14] The message of the young minister espousing joy in resignation in the picturesque and "sleepy" village of Klein-Ingersheim clearly belongs in a *Biedermeier* Germany.

Although literary critics have given less attention to it, there is another literature characteristic of this period. This is a literature designed to destroy Germany's sleep, and it is designated by the term *Pre-March*. One of the most talented authors of this type of literature was Pastor Weidig's coauthor, Georg Büchner, who along with Heinrich Heine and Ludwig Börne (1786–1837) inspired the authors grouped with him under the name Young Germany. This term has both political and literary meanings, as has been seen, because the group was first publicly named by the Frankfurt Diet in 1835 when it banned the works of the group on the occasion of the publication of Karl Gutzkow's novel *Wally the Skeptic*. Even mention of the writings of this group was considered a political crime.

As a cultural designation, Young Germany was used both by contemporaries and by later historians to cover a host of like intellectuals and writers. Georg Büchner, David Friedrich Strauss, and Friedrich Engels (1820–95) have all been listed with Heinrich Heine, Karl Gutzkow, and the others whose writings were banned in 1835.[15] Engels, who had been only fifteen when the ban was issued, wrote later: "This group of writers . . . is trying to infuse the flesh and blood of the German nation with the ideas of our century: the emancipation of

Jews and the slaves, universal constitutionalism. . . . Their ideas are not unlike the direction of my own mind."[16] Strauss, on the other hand, although willing to defend the Young Germans of 1835, did not aspire to be counted among them. His friend and fellow left-wing Hegelian Friedrich Vischer (1807–87) wrote a "defense" of Strauss motivated in part by Wolfgang Menzel's inclusion of the biblical scholar in the ranks of the political-literary criminals.[17] But whether the pastor-scholar from Würtemberg wished it or not, his work does belong with that of the Young Germans because it, together with Gutzkow's novel, disturbed the sleep of *Biedermeier* Germany in 1835.

The Life of Jesus and *Wally the Skeptic* appeared in German history in a time marked not only by an increasing gulf between economic forces and political structure but also by a cultural break. Many of the leaders of German letters, philosophy, and religion died shortly before 1835—the romantic author and theoretician Friedrich Schlegel in 1829, the philosopher Hegel in 1831, the writer Johann Wolfgang Goethe in 1832, and the theologian Schleiermacher in 1834.

Karl Lebrecht Immermann (1796–1840), often listed as a Young German himself, wrote about the passing of the older generation and its relationship to the decline of aristocratic power in an 1835 novel, *Die Epigonen*.[18] This title is taken from the Greek word meaning "descendent" or "those who come after." To this basic meaning Immermann's novel added the connotation of "a mediocre generation following one of great brilliance, condemned to imitation and amorphousness."[19] For those left behind in the 1830s the members of the brilliant generation symbolized either political retrogression or progress. Both Strauss and Gutzkow, for example, admired the attempts of Hegel and Schleiermacher to reconcile religious tradition and modernity. Insofar as these two followed their masters from the golden generation in seeking to reform Christianity to address modernity, they were bound to clash with those who wanted to return to a pre-Enlightenment Christianity and thus dethrone the cultural geniuses of the early nineteenth century. On the other hand, all of those giants had thrived, or at least survived, in a political environment which seemed retrogressive to those, like Gutzkow, who publicly avowed reform leading toward representative government. The generation left in 1835, seen by many as "condemned to imitation" or to sleep in the shadow of the dead giants, experienced the ambiguous political meanings of its cultural heritage. Heine expressed this ambiguity in 1833:

The gods are dying. Goethe is dead. He died on March 22 of last year, the momentous year when our earth lost its greatest names. It is as if in this year Death suddenly became an aristocrat, as if he wanted to distinguish particularly the notables of this earth by sending them to the grave at the same time. . . . Or, on the contrary, did Death try last year to favor democracy by destroying with the great names their authority as well and promoting intellectual equality? . . . Last year not a single king died. The gods are dying;—but we keep the kings.[20]

The Politicizing of Religious Allegiance

While young intellectuals like Gutzkow questioned how the achievements of the most creative minds of early-nineteenth-century German theologians and philosophers related to the changing social and economic order, the forces of restoration were forging their own answer. Ernst Troeltsch (1865–1923), a theologian and social scientist, found that answer reflected in Immermann's account in 1835 of the cultural and political changes that accompanied the death of the generation of Hegel and Schleiermacher. Troeltsch wrote:

The spirit of rationalism had already faded and changed itself in part into a democratic opposition, in part into capitalistic enterprise. The humanistic individualism of a romantic and classical type endured longer. But the old relationships of power and class had only been weakened, not eliminated [by the cultural forces of rationalism and humanism]. From behind [the facade of an altered culture], the power structure of a military-bureaucratic monarchy forced itself into the foreground. This structure was bound together with the restoration of a dogmatic Christian ecclesiasticism which took every opportunity to establish itself.[21]

It was precisely this dogmatic Christian ecclesiasticism, as it fought for and achieved political influence in Germany, especially in Prussia, the leading Protestant state, and as it countered the cultural forces of rationalism and humanism, that provided the context for the violent reaction to *The Life of Jesus* and *Wally the Skeptic.*

The theology of dogmatic ecclesiasticism in Pre-March Germany, a hybrid of orthodoxy and Pietism, was formed when a revival of the emphasis on adherence to traditional Lutheran dogmas as the mark of authentic Christian faith was coupled with the Pietist stress on the inner relationship of the believer to Christ, a relationship found in the heart, not the mind.[22] The name given to the historical roots of that politically influential union of Pietism and orthodoxy is the Awakening.[23] A reaction to the Enlightenment, this lay movement advocated "a return to a piety based on a simple faith, the Bible, and Christian fellowship." At the close of the eighteenth century and throughout the first third of the nineteenth, it spread throughout Germany.[24] Figures such as Johann Georg Hamann (1730–88) and Heinrich Jung-Stilling (1740–1817), who advocated a biblical Christianity divorced from rationalism, provided models for what was to become a religious attitude characterized by a biblical emotionalism that expressed itself not only in worship but in social and political arenas. Although the Awakening had various shapes in the different regions of Germany, it was most significant for providing "the spiritual basis for that emphasis upon Christian principles in the social order characteristic of the Restoration."[25] This conservative direction of religious renewal was fixed in the 1830s when it became the "official" religious style of the ecclesiastical and political leaders of Prussia.

It is not difficult to understand why Friedrich Weidig's proclamation of the revolutionary demand of the Word of God landed him in prison in 1834. In that year, however, Strauss had advanced from his small-town pastorate to a junior academic post at Tübingen. After 1830 he was to be found not in underground groups plotting or training for the overthrow of repressive government but rather in Berlin, where he studied the thought of Hegel and Schleiermacher. In other words,

Strauss was following an innocuous course, studying the theological and philosophical ideas of respected German masters and addressing himself as a theological scholar among scholars to questions raised by their intellectual programs to express the meaning of Christianity in the modern age. In fact, by 1834 he was on the threshold of a high position in the Restoration establishment, possibly even one at the University of Berlin. However, Berlin was becoming the university of Hengstenberg, rather than of Hegel or of Schleiermacher, and it would have no room for the author of a biblical criticism that questioned the historicity of the gospel narratives. In fact, even less extreme attempts at the reform of Christianity, which sought only to reconcile its literal and traditional forms with modern thought, were becoming suspect as dangerous to the state as well as to simple Christian belief. As Bigler has put it:

In 1815–1848—as during the Reformation—political ideas and attitudes became associated with theological creeds. The government no longer looked upon controversies between theology professors as mere "parsons' quarrels" (*Pfaffengezäl*) as it had done under monarchial absolutism in the seventeenth and eighteenth centuries. Since in the midst of changing political conditions after 1815 the theology professors continued to play a crucial role in clerical personnel recruitment—by training, examining, and recommending candidates for church positions—there resulted an increased attention by the government to the creed and political leanings of prospective appointees to the university, and its policy favored men who could be expected to support the ruling authorities.[26]

Pastors' Quarrels and Political Ideology

Not all theological arguments of the seventeenth and eighteenth centuries had been ignored by governmental powers as pastors' quarrels. The most famous of those arguments prefigured that engendered by *The Life of Jesus*. The stellar figure of the German Enlightenment, Gotthold Ephraim Lessing (1728–81), became the subject of a public dispute in the late eighteenth century when he published excerpts from the writings of Hermann Samuel Reimarus (1696–1768). Reimarus, a teacher in Hamburg, who knew his studies would arouse controversy and thus did not seek to publish them himself, left a work comparing the four gospel accounts of the events in the life of Jesus. This comparison highlighted the inconsistencies in the gospel reports of these events and raised questions about their historical accuracy, as well as about the truthfulness of the evangelists. Simply put, Reimarus forcefully presented the case that at least some of the reports "lied." Lessing brought his findings to light in the *Wolfenbüttal Fragments* (1774–78).

Lessing maintained that honest, open questioning need not destroy Christian faith because the truth of Christian faith can be affirmed without the historical verification of the gospel texts. That truth has its authentic verification not in history but in reason. Eighteenth-century Brunswick was not ready for Lessing's enlightenment on the historicity of the life story of Jesus. Because of the violent criticism that Lessing drew, the government of Brunswick banned all of his theological writings.

Johann Melchior Goeze (1717–86), an orthodox Lutheran pastor, was Lessing's most virulent opponent. His vibrantly expressed opposition to an enlightened criticism and interpretation of Christianity is classically representative of one type of union between traditionalism in religion and conservatism in politics. Goeze wrote:

> [Lessing] believes that he does the Christian Religion and our Saviour a service, and promotes the honor of both, when he serves as a midwife in publishing the most scandalous pamphlets directed against both. Does Mr. Lessing not see—or does he not want to see—*the logical consequences of this principle*? What would he reply to someone who says: The system of government practiced by the best and most just of rulers does not deserve allegiance until every conceivable—however stupid—objection against the system and every conceivable libel and insult directed against the person of the ruler, has been set out in print, and placed in the hands of the mass of his subjects; until his most virtuous and benevolent actions have been provoked into defending the honor of their Master, his system of government and his actions?[28]

Here Goeze spelled out a logical parallel between biblical criticism and political criticism. Taking another step, he extended that parallelism to the sphere of social mores. He asked: "What would Lessing reply to someone who asserts: The true nature of chastity, and the duty to preserve it and to resist all tendencies toward filth cannot be clearly illumined, nor adequately established until every piece of pornography has been distributed, rare items have been reprinted, foreign items translated and those still in manuscript put into print?"[29]

Clearly, Goeze was challenging Lessing's conviction that admission and investigation of doubt would not hurt Christianity. But at the heart of this eighteenth-century pastor's reaction to Lessing was the issue of the right to doubt. In effect, he objected to a principle that would allow every conceivable objection against a system to be set out in print and placed in the hands of the mass of peasants. Thus this theological quarrel over the relation of human reason to biblical text was also a social and political quarrel over freedom of expression and freedom of the press. Goeze believed that a critical approach to the Bible carried social and political implications and that the "proper" order of the religious, political, and social realms was strengthened not by criticism but by protection from doubt and temptation.

Theological Rationalism and Restoration Politics

The outstanding spokesperson for the "proper" order of the religious and political realms in 1835 was the Berlin theology professor Hengstenberg, who became the most important leader of the counterrevolutionary forces in the 1840s. Through the *Evangelical Church Newspaper*, which he not only edited but also frequently contributed articles to, his influence spread far beyond the circle of his students in Berlin. Moreover, he expressed the views of a large segment of the powerful Prussian aristocracy, the Junkers, who espoused a simple, biblical Christian faith and who fought hard for the restoration of their feudal privilege.

In the 1830s, Hengstenberg led a revival of the identification between a rationalist interpretation of Christianity and the potential for political disloyalty first made by his eighteenth-century orthodox brother Goeze. This church leader opposed not only the rationalism that challenged traditional Christian belief but also the clearly *Christian* rationalism that used reason to support the tenets of faith. Formulated in large measure by Christian Wolff (1679–1754), this form of rationalism had dominated theological training in Germany in the early nineteenth century, but it had fallen from favor by the 1830s, in part because many proponents of restoration suspected any form of rationalism of carrying revolutionary potential.

By the time that Gutzkow and Strauss resurrected the specter of Lessing, theological rationalism had been on the wane for a decade, having been supplanted in the universities by the mediating theology of Schleiermacher, the speculative theology of Hegel, and the neoorthodox theology of Hengstenberg. How could a revival of theological rationalism, even in its "critical" form, cause such a disturbance when its strength as an intellectual position was nearly gone?

As the social historian Hans Rosenberg explains, concepts outlive their use by intellectual leaders, and an intellectual movement often reaches the peak of its influence after it has been replaced by a new theory. In the 1830s theological rationalism had an importance in Germany far beyond the number of its adherents in theological seminaries because the pastors and church officials trained in the heyday of theological rationalism were reaching middle age and the peak of their own careers. Thus there were in the 1830s "thousands and thousands of preachers, teachers, and educated laity who had received their Christian education from rationalist theology professors."[30] Rosenberg names among these professors, along with the distinguished Heinrich E. G. Paulus (1761–1851), the lesser-known A. L. Wegscheider (1771–1849), Karl G. Bretschneider (1776–1848), Johann Philipp Gabler (1753–1826), and Friedrich von Ammon (1776–1841), the very "predecessors" who appear in the pages of *The Life of Jesus*.[31] It seems that even if Strauss had done nothing more than edit more of

Reimarus's writings, in the political and theological atmosphere of 1835 such an action would have provoked charges of treason and heresy from many in political and ecclesiastical power.

Many theology students, along with their rationalist professors, had in fact been stirred by liberal political ideals, and they had supported the reforms in government initiated or inspired by Napoleon in the early part of the nineteenth century. W. M. L. de Wette (1780–1849), a professor of biblical exegesis at the University of Berlin from 1810, became in 1819 a symbol of the extremes to which rational theology could lead when he was dismissed from the faculty for writing a sympathy letter to the mother of Karl Sand, Kotzebue's assassin. For many in Berlin, de Wette's letter was considered to be an "even greater scandal than the murder itself."[32] Hegel took care to distance himself from any suggestion of sympathy for de Wette.[33] Schleiermacher, on the other hand, defended de Wette and, for some time after the latter's dismissal from the university, was subject to the suspicions of the proponents of restoration.[34] De Wette's replacement at Berlin was Hengstenberg!

In 1830 two other "outdated" rationalists resurrected in the pages of *The Life of Jesus*, A. L. Wegscheider and W. Gesenius (1786–1842), were the principals in a public dispute at the University of Halle. These two rationalists had questioned the literal accuracy of the scripture accounts, and for this Hengstenberg, urged on by Ludwig von Gerlach, attacked them in the *Evangelical Church Newspaper*.[35] Using copies of students' notes from their lectures, Hengstenberg pointed out their theological heresy and accused them of political unreliability. To Gerlach, they exemplified the principle that criticism fosters unbelief, which in turn "encourages disrespect for the heavenly and worldly order."[36] Hengstenberg was to say that it was "sinful for a Christian student to be loyal to a rationalist teacher."[37]

Religious and political emotions of all shapes were aroused by the attack in the *Evangelical Church Newspaper* against Wegschneider and Genesius. At the time, however, the victory went to them and to the Prussian minister of education, Baron Karl Altenstein (1770–1840), who came to their defense, affirming their rights of freedom of conscience and expression. The two men kept their jobs. However, Altenstein, who had also held that "a state organ should not interfere in theological controversies,"[38] was contradicted by King Friedrich Wilhelm III (1770–1840). On 23 September 1830 the king declared: "I consider the influence of theology professors [who] do not feel bound by the dogmas of the Protestant Church [as] eternal truths [to be] extremely dangerous for the state."[39]

Thus, after 1830 it would be extremely important for theological schools to demonstrate their acceptance of orthodoxy. The political implications of schools of theology, not merely the political views of individuals, became an issue.[40] Most important for this study, theologians felt a duty to take upon themselves the task of "unveiling the hidden political meanings of their opponent's theological position,"[41] especially to defend themselves against the increasingly influential pen of the neoorthodox Pietist Hengstenberg.

From 1830 on, battle lines were drawn between neoorthodox Pietism, on the one side, and theological rationalism and liberalism, on the other. As the theological position of Hengstenberg sought and gained prominence as the "prop of the monarch," any argument against his theological position risked being construed as disloyalty.[42] Hengstenberg defended the supernatural origin of both government and the divine revelation recorded in the Bible. The assertion of the rationalist of the right of reason to judge or to supplement biblical revelation provided a basis for his opposition to it. This assertion carried egalitarian implications because it presupposed an innate human ability to reason, to progress in knowledge, and to enhance, if not transcend, the truth given to it by the authority of revelation. In the area of religion Christians so gifted, although perhaps engaged in demonstrating rather than questioning the historical truth of the gospel stories, would not necessarily be dependent on traditions in biblical interpretation or the doctrine of their denomination to attain that truth. A political conservative like Hengstenberg maintained that rationalist theology would promote a like attitude in politics—one that declared people free from the historical traditions of their home territories and capable of forming their own governments. Moreover, the July Revolution had raised the specter of violent change, not merely rational reform. Hengstenberg proclaimed that it was the "duty of the Church to reinforce the eternal foundation of government" and to fight "religious rationalism," "a form of disbelief clearly connected with liberalism and the revolt against the given order."[43]

Confronted with these accusations of the seditious political implications of the use of autonomous reason in the discussion of religion, theological rationalists and liberals defended themselves. In 1835, for example, Karl Bretschneider wrote *Theology and Revolution*, in which he gave an especially clear apology for the role of reason in theology and politics.[44] He argued that without reform revolution in politics and unbelief in religion were inevitable. He assumed that change in the conditions of culture was real and inescapable. Thus, rather than encourage revolution, a theology attuned to deal with change, to reformulate doctrine for a changing culture—that is, rationalist and liberal theology—contributed to stability and orderly progression.[45] This argument linked theological and political ideas in what can be called a typically moderate position.

Hegelian theology was in a curious position in this debate. It shared with rationalist and liberal theology the acceptance of the legitimacy of reason as a guide to truth, but it was also the child of a political philosopher whose system seemed also to be a prop of the monarchy. Menzel, who at the time that he fought Gutzkow and Strauss was a moderate, explained the position of Hegel's philosophy in the satiric model he shared with one of his enemies, Heine: "Hegel's philosophy would yet have excited but little attention if it had not gained political adherents and supporters. How? Has not the God-professor looked proudly down upon the kings of this world? I know not; but it is certain that attendance upon the lectures of Hegel has been strongly recommended—that his disciples were always selected for public appointments."[46]

Menzel was referring to the fact that the Prussian minister of education, Altenstein, and the architect of the Prussian educational system, Johannes Schulze (1786–1869), admired Hegel's philosophy and found in it a justification for the bureaucracy they headed. During the 1830s they promoted the appointment of many Hegelians in Prussian educational institutions.[47] Menzel also explained why, in his opinion, Hegel's philosophy was useful to those in power:

> The doctrine of Hegel offered itself as a political scholasticism, equipped almost with the same means as the old ecclesiastical scholasticism. As men had *to do not with matters of fact, not with demonstration, but only with ideas*, when they drew nothing from religion or moral doctrines, but everything from logic alone, they could then play with ideas and propositions as they pleased, and prove everything or nothing. The doctrine became a system of absolute dialectics without substance, without object, a mere means of explaining as they pleased. To this purpose is the notorious proposition of Hegel, "all that is, is rational," made use of to show that the present condition is the most rational, and that it is not merely revolutionary, but eminently stupid, foolish and unphilosophical, to take any exceptions to it.[48]

An attempt made by a young Hegelian to reconcile Christianity with modernity by demonstrating its truth with a logic that transcended that of petty rationalism could have expected to find approbation in the atmosphere satirized by Menzel. In 1835, although Hengstenberg's star was on the rise and his own opposition to rationalism extended to Hegelian theology, Altenstein and even the king saw in Hegel's philosophy a potential justification of monarchy in politics and orthodoxy in religion. But the young Hegelian who made such an attempt, Strauss, insisted upon dealing with "matters of fact, with demonstrations"—with testing the validity of the gospel narratives—and he found no approbation from the Hegelians in Berlin. Rather, *The Life of Jesus* would bring the political implications of Hegelian philosophy into question.

The Life of Jesus, as well as *Wally the Skeptic*, appeared in the midst of a growing confrontation between conservative and moderate political and theological forces. When they entered on the scene, they did more than add to the ranks of the rationalist and liberal expressions espousing freedom of thought and progressive change. In their own way both books were products of the postrationalist intellectual tradition, and as such they did more than raise the stakes in a "right-center" conflict. They helped change the game so that, for a while at least, the "left" became an important player. These books gave new expression to the yearning for freedom felt by many in their authors' generation in a form that carried political meaning. This form of expression was irony; its political implication was democracy.

The Life of Jesus revived the issues at stake in the Lessing affair and evoked responses that utilized the logic of Goeze's associations of Christianity, politics, and social-sexual mores. Indeed, Strauss seemed to have escaped the fate of the *epigonen* of 1835 by leaping back behind the apparently more gentle giants of the intervening generation and resurrecting the memory of the Father of the German Enlightenment. As one nineteenth-century theologian observed of the reaction to *The Life of Jesus*: "Not since the time of the *Wolfenbüttal Fragments* and the polemical writings of their famous editor [Lessing] had the theological world been set in similar agitation."[49]

The Young German Gutzkow's *Wally the Skeptic* also revived the Goeze-Lessing issues. In fact, Gutzkow set out consciously to recapture Lessing's power to agitate theological orthodoxy and the political and social order that sought to be strengthened by it. The year before he wrote *Wally the Skeptic*, he had wanted to take up where Lessing left off and continue to edit the writings of Reimarus, but he had known that Metternich's censors would block his project. Gutzkow used the novel form to create the effect that reading Reimarus would have had on the public. The presence of the *Fragments* in *Wally the Skeptic* is not subtle. Gutzkow's heroine reads them and says: "There is a lot of dust on the book, many old Franconian elements, but I have brushed this off and gained from my reading a very modern interpretation. The author is supposed to be . . . Reimarus. His complete examination of Christianity stands in a glass case in the Hamburg library. They don't want to publish the book. They fear that moths will fly out of the yellowed pages of that critique and gnaw on Christianity itself."[50] In fact, criticism of the historicity of the gospel narratives, criticism of social-sexual mores, and criticism of politics are all explicit in *Wally the Skeptic*. The Federal Diet did not have to exercise complex hermeneutical processes to see that this novel set out to undermine existing social relationships.

In *The Life of Jesus*, on the other hand, only the criticism of the historicity of the gospel narratives is explicit, yet figures such as Menzel, the literary critic, and Hengstenberg, the theologian, found in the book not only religious heresy but also immorality and political treachery. The logic of pre-1789, pre-Napoleonic Brunswick was alive again in 1835. The categorization of *The Life of Jesus* with *Wally the Skeptic* as a pornographic book was not an aberrant act of theological or political fanatics. It represented an astute assessment of the theological book's potential to disturb "throne and altar" and the society supported by their union.

The absence of the left as a significant player in the German political scene was, of course, in large measure due to the success of the repression of dissent by the Restoration powers. After 1815 the sharp contrast between aristocracy and democracy, introduced into Germany by the French Revolution, had been muted even among those desirous of constitutional representative government. Those liberals, especially the ones like Menzel who had their homes in Strauss's own south Germany, had sought to bridge aristocracy and democracy in some sort of constitutional monarchy that retained distinctions between groups of people. They did oppose the special privilege and form of hereditary aristocracy, but as Menzel made so clear, they admired an aristocracy of feeling and virtue that they understood to be rooted in a noble German past.

After 1830, however, the stark contrast between aristocracy and democracy was revived in the rhetoric of those inspired by the Paris Revolution to seek more immediate change in Germany. On the one hand, in Prussia an amalgamation of hereditary aristocracy and hereditary monarchial power with ecclesiastical leaders was becoming solidified, thus providing a historical example of how aristocracy could distance itself from democracy. On the other hand, the Paris Revolution revived the ideal of an untainted democracy.[51] In 1832, Heine wrote: "All constitutions, even the best, will fail to help us, so long as the aristocracy has not been destroyed down to its last remaining root."[52]

Despite Menzel's total disparagement of Hegel's political position, there were elements in Hegel's political philosophy that were similar to those in south German liberalism. Hegel did advocate a *constitutional* monarchy, and in 1820 in his *Philosophy of Right* he wrote: "Equally inadequate is the mass of contemporary talk about the democratic and aristocratic elements in monarchy, because when the elements specified in such talk are found in a monarchy there is no longer anything democratic or aristocratic about them."[53] According to the philosopher, the unity of a *true* state, which is necessarily a monarchy, headed by *one* man, is such that the distinction between its being grounded in the hereditary rights or special gifts of the few or in the natural rights of all was a meaningless one.

Like *Wally the Skeptic*, Strauss's *Life of Jesus* would introduce democratic sentiments into German cultural life in the wake of the Paris Revolution. Because *The Life of Jesus* did so as a Hegelian statement, its effects were not as easy to eliminate as were those of the novel. Hegel's theory of the monarchy, as well as his theory about Christ, would be unmasked as containing at its core democratic implications that posed a direct threat to the union of throne and altar, which in the Prussia of the mid-1830s was also the union of monarchy and aristocracy.

Chapter Three ❖ Irony ❖ The Holy Principle of Spiritual Freedom

In his 1833 essay "The Romantic School," Heine made what on the surface seems to be a politically innocuous aesthetic judgment on the advocate of irony and author of *Puss in Boots* (1797), Ludwig Tieck (1759–1837). He judged that, despite the similarities that many critics saw between the comedies of Tieck and those of Aristophanes, Tieck's work fell short of that greatness. In explanation, Heine wrote: "Our German Aristophanes [have] abstained from any exalted philosophy of life; with great modesty they held their tongues about the two most important conditions of man, the political and the religious."[1]

Heine was not the only German intellectual who criticized a German literature for being abstracted from political and religious conditions; nor was he the only one who yearned for a genuine German Aristophanes.[2] Nearly thirty years earlier, Hegel himself had made an association between the plays of Aristophanes and the political freedom of the Greek people in *The Phenomenology of Spirit* (1807).[3] In 1826, August von Platen (1796–1835) wrote that "only a free people is capable of producing an Aristophanes."[4] Heine repeated this opinion by linking the absence of Aristophanian comedy in the 1820s and 1830s to "the lack of political freedom in Germany." He elaborated: "We Germans, who possessed almost no serious political newspapers, were always doubly blessed with a host of [a]esthetic journals containing nothing but worthless fairy tales and theatrical reviews."[5] For a brief moment after the July Revolution of 1830 overt political writing surfaced, but owing to the efficiency of the censorship of the Federal Diet religion and politics had once again given way in the newspapers to the topic of "theater criticism."[6] *Wally the Skeptic* and *The Life of Jesus* were to alter this state of affairs.

In *Wally the Skeptic* the heroine and her friend-lover, Caesar, do not hold their tongues about religion and politics. In what

Leo Löwenthal describes as "perhaps the first modern conversation between members of middle class society," Wally and Caesar tease and banter about serious and trivial things, emotional and economic matters, as though they were all of the same import.[7] Wally asks Caesar:

"Why do you stop short of talking about politics?"
"In Athens no popular orator was allowed to appear unless married."
"How erudite you are! I am too—in Crete no one could make laws unless he had a rope around his neck."
"That's the same law—the Athenians actually meant those who had no such ropes around their necks."
"How improper!"
"Wally!"

Soon the topic of conversation shifts to travel, and Wally observes:

"The Rhine steamers go too fast."
"They go too slowly and tire your eyes. The idea of a fiery turtle creeping across the water is part of our imagination, and we have simply become accustomed to considering the creeping slow."
"That's a strange image! I wonder what my aunt [in the adjacent room] is laughing about so loudly."
"Your aunt is a spider creeping over the ocean."
"What makes you say that?"
"She's speculating in stocks."
"She's talking politics. It's all beyond me."
"If it were within your grasp, you'd resemble a butterfly which had strayed into the gas-lit confusion of a drawing room."
"Butterflies have been overused as analogies."
"Like immortality itself."

Wally is shaken a bit at what she takes to be Caesar's disdain of permanence or fidelity, and she comments:

"You aren't a Christian?"
"Do you believe that Christ rose from the dead?"
"Oh, God, never mind, I can't think about it."[8]

Whether or not this dialogue is worthy of Aristophanes, judging from the violent reaction it evoked, it must have borne some of the power of the politically effective plays of the Greek author. One of the informants who reported to Metternich wrote: "The effects of reading Gutzkow's *Wally* are becoming more and more apparent among the lower classes and in public places. At the inn of Zöller . . . there was recently present a journeyman who had read *Wally* and was making a comparison between Gutzkow and the reformer Luther. The journeyman observed that Gutzkow and his friends wanted to introduce a new religion, which certainly seemed a reasonable idea to him."[9] It did not seem like a reasonable idea to Metternich or Hengstenberg, or even to liberals like Menzel—or, as it turned out, to the innkeeper Zöller, who purportedly threw the advocate of *Wally* out of his establishment.

After Gutzkow's trial, not many public advocates of *Wally the Skeptic* were to be found. Similarly, in the midst of the expressions of "panic-stricken terror" and the innumerable more constrained forms of censure directed at *The Life of Jesus*, not many theologians came to its defense. What defense the theology book did have was provided almost entirely by Strauss himself. Even Ruge did not take up the case of *The Life of Jesus* enthusiastically until after the first round of defense was put forth by Strauss alone. A principal charge against the book was, of course, that it was marked by the same characteristics—immorality, heresy, and cynicism—as those found in *Wally the Skeptic*. Instead of defending his book against this accusation, Strauss did what few of his fellow Germans would: he defended *Wally the Skeptic*. He admitted to a commonality between the books, and influenced by his friend and fellow Hegelian Vischer, who would become one of the outstanding aestheticians of the nineteenth century, he identified that commonality as irony. Moreover, Strauss associated the literary and theological writers' right to use irony with political attitudes.

Strauss's writings about irony in defense of *The Life of Jesus* were an astute interpretation of the book, not a guide to his original intentions. Of course he did not consciously intend to write a political treatise or even to structure his theological treatise as irony. But Strauss and Vischer identified the element of irony in Hegel's philosophy, and they defended its expression as a duty and right in their age. They wrote what was in effect a left-wing Hegelian defense of irony. Placed in the context of the literary atmosphere of the 1830s, this defense is revealing of the structure of *The Life of Jesus* that carried political meaning.

The Literary Atmosphere of the 1830s: Menzel and the Young Germans

In *The Eclipse of Biblical Narrative*, Hans W. Frei saw a relationship between German biblical hermeneutics and the fact that in the early nineteenth century Germany, unlike England and France, did not have a tradition of narrative fiction in which "internal character development" was balanced by a "portrayal of the external social world."[10] Early-nineteenth-century German literary critics in the traditions of Classicism and Romanticism disparaged such fiction in the name of a superior German literature concerned with "poetic" form and "ideas" defined either as inner, subjective truth or as objective, transcendent truth. Following Erich Auerbach, Frei associated the lack of realism in German letters with its social and political condition, specifically its lack of a substantive and effective middle class and the division of Germany into a number of separate political territories.[11] Moreover, a pattern of petty despotism and paternalism existed in most of the small, disunited territories. This pattern allowed the ordinary German little political activity, and thus he or she did not experience himself or herself as an *agent* in history. In France and England, on the other hand, substantial minorities had gained political influence.[12] Furthermore, national unity and economic advancement provided the conditions in those countries for the development of realism, for the literary descriptions of the "interaction of human beings with the upheavals of large-scale and historical forces."[13] In Germany ideas and ideals, not historical action, constituted the realm of freedom and dominated literary style.

What is significant about these observations for our purposes is that by the 1830s, German Classicism and Romanticism were being criticized in a demand for a new type of literature that would be comparable to that of other nations.[14] The most influential, if not the most profound, literary critic and historian to make this demand was Wolfgang Menzel. His *German Literature* (1828; revised in 1836) was immensely popular throughout Europe in its day and had a lasting influence not only on subsequent interpretations of German literary history but also on the development of a German national literature itself.[15] With his enemies in 1835, the Young Germans, he shared the conviction that the state of literature was dependent on the conditions of social and political life.[16] For Menzel and the true literary founders of Young Germany, Heinrich Heine and Ludwig Börne, the source of this view was precisely that heightened political awareness and expectation derived from the wars of liberation against France and from their own involvement in the *Burschenschaft* movement. Menzel and the Young Germans agreed that politically Germany trailed England and France, lacking national unity and freedoms for the people, and furthermore that its literature, particularly that of its greatest writer, Goethe (1749–1832), was a correlate of this condition. But they disagreed not only about the meaning of present conditions in German social and political life but also on the form that a new literature ought to take. Their debate centered on the issue of what it meant to "portray the external social world" and on the value of the historical novel, which had great popularity in Germany at the time.

In *German Literature*, Menzel declared that the classical age of Goethe and Schiller, as well as the romantic age of Schlegel, had passed, but that Restoration Germany had produced no new literary form of its own. Instead, it had been seized by "Anglomania," a mark of which was fascination with the historical novels of Walter Scott. In his opinion, Scott made "almost greater conquests among the German public than in England," and he found more imitators among German writers than English.[17] German writers "hammer[ed] the leather on Walter Scott's last," and although the products, aside from those of

Willibald Alexis (1798–1871) and a handful of others, were not necessarily excellent, "every semi-annual fair [brought] out from eighty to a hundred historical novels."[18]

Menzel thought that this fascination was healthy for Germany because "the style of the historical novel is suited to a manly nation" and to an awakened interest in the great, moving political events that pulled the Germans away from their sleep in the "bosom of peace and family."[19] The historical novel, in his definition, takes a literary form that stands in "a very close relation to historical composition"; the novel uses the same materials as history writing, differing only in the fact that it "regards particularly the beautiful, or only the interesting and the enchanting,—whereas strict history, on the contrary, looks to the true, independent of everything that pleases."[20] The historical novel is "democratic" in form, in contrast to the drama, in which "man stands up free, beyond the range of history, and fighting against it," and to the epic, in which "the deity disposes of history from beyond it." In the historical novel "man is only a product of history," but in such a way that he is seen as a blossom "which vegetates from the midst of it, nourished by its sap, and held fast by its secret powers."[21] In this literary form divinity is present as the nourishing soil of history, but works no miracles.

Menzel also contrasted the historical novel to the domestic and provincial forms of some of Restoration literature and to the apolitical and ahistorical content of Goethe's writings. He concluded that German literature in the nineteenth century had to "emulate history"; it had to "adopt the historical element" just as tenaciously as it had adopted the "philosophical" in the eighteenth century.[22] This philosophical element, which arises out of the characteristic reflective nature of the German people, is positive, but as it was exercised in the eighteenth century it was insufficient because it corresponded to a failure of action, of manliness. Goethe is the literary representative of the failures of this age; he is the representative of effeminacy, political indifference, immorality, and aristocracy. His most famous novel, *Wilhelm Meister*, was nothing more than a chronicle of his own ego, which wanted to know no bounds. In his powerful rhetoric, Menzel stated: "But Goethe's age is past, never to return. . . . Goethe's profoundest doctrine, which he laid down in Wilhelm Meister's indenture, was 'Seriousness surprises.' Yes: it must surprise those who, taken up with sports and dreams have paid no attention to the realities about them."[23]

But if Goethe's age was past, some of the marks of his writing were reappearing in the literature of the Young Germans, whom Menzel treated under the heading of "Gallomania," the interest in things French which followed "Anglomania." Along with immorality, their writings showed if not political indifference then a traitorous attitude. Menzel, of course, also saw effeminacy in Gutzkow's *Wally the Skeptic.*[24] To him the duty of writers was to find the "fruitfulness" of the future in the apparent sleep of the Germany of the present. The literary enemies of this endeavor were the Young Germans, who could only criticize the moral, religious, and political conditions in Germany.[25] As we have seen, he made sure that these literary enemies of progress were also declared its political enemies.

Menzel and the Young Germans both sought political changes in Germany that would lead toward some kind of more participatory government, and they used their pens to stir the public to political awareness. For Menzel "historical, democratic" writing would serve to remind the people of their glorious past and their present capabilities for action. The Young Germans, however, chose the means of a direct confrontation with what they thought were the intolerable conditions of the present. Thus, although both programs gave a central place to the socially responsible novel, they differed on the proper form for this type of novel. For example, Ludolf Wienbarg, as opposed to Menzel, welcomed the decline of interest in Germany in the historical novel. He considered the novels of Walter Scott to be only an "anodyne."[26] In fact, in Immermann's *Die Epigonen*, Scott's form of realism is satirized in a scene in which an aristocratic woman, inspired by Scott's novels, decides to recreate a tournament in honor of her husband. This imitation of heroic history results in the comic revelation of the ineptness of the noblemen to execute the deeds of their ancestors. Only a circus performer possesses the dexterity to recreate the past.[27]

Wienbarg also noted that England and France were losing interest in historical novels in favor of critical social novels, such as those of Balzac. It is precisely this kind of writing that Wienbarg thought would become dominant in Germany and for which Gutzkow's *Wally*, for all the stylistic defects he admitted it had, was a precursor.[28] Thus, in opposition to their predecessors, the Young German literary voices espoused a narrative fiction similar to the literature that Frei names "realistic." The Young Germans, however, made a distinction not made by Frei between the narrative fiction of such writers as Scott and what they saw as the socially critical and thus "realistic" narrative fiction of such writers as Balzac. George Lukács describes this distinction by pointing out that Scott did not raise the "social questions of contemporary England in his novels." In contrast to Scott, Balzac, who was himself influenced, as were the Young Germans, by the July Revolution, "passes from the portrayal of past history to the portrayal of the present as history," that is, as capable of being altered.[29]

The Young Germans sought a form of literature which could effectively confront the intolerable conditions of present social and political life, and they rejected a form of realism that was either a retreat to the past or a copy of present reality. In the epilogue to *Wally the Skeptic* Gutzkow wrote: "Possibility, that realm of shadows that lies behind the visible manifestations in the light of events, is an endless realm. There is a world which, even if it only exists in our dreams, could just as easily be pieced together to form reality. Like reality itself, a world which we are capable of deducing through imagination and trust. Shallow minds are only aware of what happens; gifted minds sense what could be; free minds construct their own world."[30] He described the unflattering comparisons being made between English and German letters and the pressure on German writers to imitate the English writers' ability to "copy reality."[31] In contrast to this copy, he said, "a truth of poetry is arising that nothing in the institutions surrounding us corresponds to, *an ideal opposition*, a poetic opposite of our times that will have to withstand a double attack, . . . against the poetry of reality which has so many adherents among poets and critics."[32]

In one critic's opinion the action of the censors in 1835 in repressing the writings of Gutzkow and his group could well have changed the course of German letters, delaying the production of excellent realistic narrative fictional form for decades.[33] What is important here, however, is Gutzkow's attempt to confront the present in *Wally the Skeptic* and the form of expression that his writing assumed. Strauss and Vischer defended his attempt, and they gave the name of irony to Gutzkow's mode of realism.[34]

The Aesthetics of Strauss and Vischer: The Modernization of Hegel

When placed in the company of such dramatically public figures as Menzel and Gutzkow, the young scholars Strauss and Vischer, immersed as they were in struggling with the meaning of the Hegelian Idea in theology and aesthetics, seem to belong to another age. Clearly their basically Hegelian aesthetic principle was drawn from another age, that of German Classicism.[35] They held that art is a manifestation of the beautiful, defined as the sensuous appearance of the idea.[36] Hegel's version of the principle declared that the artistic mode of sensuous representation (*Vorstellung*) was able to reveal "to consciousness and to bring to utterance the divine nature, the deepest interests of humanity, and the most comprehensive truths of mind."[37] How such a view could support a defense of those demanding a literature in the service of contemporary politics is not immediately evident. But Strauss, following Vischer, was not a slavish disciple of Hegel in aesthetics.[38] Moreover, Hegel himself had linked the Classicist's definition of art with historical development and thus to social and political forms.[39]

Basically, the two Hegelians held that Menzel's judgment on *Wally the Skeptic* was invalid because he applied to the work, especially to the nude scene, *extrinsic* criteria in the form of moral laws, in particular the rigid code of the moral discipline of the Turners, the prototype of the *Burschenschaften*, rather than recognize that form and ethical content (the beautiful and the good) cannot be judged separately.[40] These Hegelians, in contrast to many Classicists, saw "the beautiful" not as a static concept but rather as a description of a form that immediately embodied the actual content of the conditions of human life common to all. In a move away from Hegel, however, they defended a form that he found neither "beautiful" nor capable of bearing ethical content. That form was irony, "the holy principle of spiritual freedom," as Vischer called it.[41] In fact, Vischer well knew that Hegel had declared himself the enemy of irony in his lectures on aesthetics, and the young scholar had set out to prove him wrong. Strauss praised Vischer's "bettering of the old man," commenting that in the rejection of irony Hegel had shown himself to be a "philistine,"[42] defined by Heine as "a cowardly burgher who hinders progress, and acknowledges every existing authority, nay, more, identifies himself with it."[43] The irony that Strauss and Vischer upheld against the philistine Hegel was that of the Romantic Friedrich Schlegel.

Hegel had defined Schlegel's irony as a negativity that asserted "the nothingness of all that is objective." Schlegel's irony was "that concentration of the I into itself for which all bounds are broken, and which only endeavors to live in the bliss of self-enjoyment." The mark of irony in the artistic work was the depiction of the "divine as ironical," as the "self-annihilation of what is noble, great and excellent." Thus irony was different from comedy, which, "on the contrary, brings to nothing what is in itself null, a false and self-contradictory phenomenon."[44] Hegel maintained that true character in the subjects of art had to possess seriousness and a "substantial interest": that is, the ability to become absorbed in and adhere to a purpose, a truth, a morality which has value independent of the self.[45] From his discussion of irony it would seem that Hegel and Menzel, in spite of their vastly differing approaches to art, might have agreed on what were good works.

Vischer, however, would not let the "old man" forget his own youth in the age of Schlegel. He maintained that in *The Phenomenology of Spirit* Hegel had articulated Schlegel's concept of irony in his own description of comedy.[46] There Hegel had described the fulfillment and end of what he called the religion of art, exemplified in classical Greek art and religion, as taking place in comedy. In this "absolute" art, the substantial, that truth outside of and objective to the self, took the form of ethical spirit, the spirit of a free nation, "in which custom and order constitute the common substance of all, whose reality and existence each and everyone knows to be his own will and his own deed."[47] This sense of individual unity with a common ethical and objective substance, which Hegel also called the *actual* spirit, provided the ground for the production of art in its "absolute form." This was an art in which there is an immediate union of the sensuous with the idea. It was seen in its most perfect in the statues of the Greek gods, but it was also manifested in all the anthropomorphisms of "absolute power" in Greek epics and tragedies.[48]

In Greek comedy, at its peak in the plays of Aristophanes, however, the gods as representations of ethical, objective, actual spirit are negated "by the force of the individual self." Through irony, in which the actors representing the fate of the gods take off their masks and reveal their commonness and sameness with the audience, self-consciousness beholds "that whatever assumes the form of essentiality as against self-consciousness, is instead dissolved within it—within its thought, its existence and acts—and is quite at its mercy."[49] Substantial reality outside the self is lost, and that loss corresponds to the decline of the Greek state.

In the *Phenomenology* the collapse of the religion of art and the advent of comedy prepare the way not for a new art but for Absolute religion. The state of spiritual good health experienced after comedy soon becomes an unsatisfied yearning for something substantial outside the self. However, consciousness now knows that it can embrace substantiality only in a form that is adequate to self-consciousness itself. Such a substantiality appears no more in art but in Christ, the incarnation of the Divine Being, the content of "Absolute religion."[50] Here consciousness does not set out from its own inner life and in itself combine the thought of God, the Idea, with existence as it did in the Greek religion of art. It now encounters something outside the self, "from immediate present existence, and recognizes God in it." One might say that for the Hegel of the *Phenomenology* Christ is the end of art.[51] He is the resolution of that yearning of the soul produced by comic irony.[52]

Vischer not only found Schlegel's definition of irony as the "self-annihilation of what is truly great," in Hegel's description of comedy but went so far as to say that the belief in the incarnation of Christ is the ground for the justification of comic irony in modern literature.[53] In fact, Vischer implied that Christianity had served to confirm the truth revealed by Greek comedy, that "the subject is the power which has all content in itself, and next to which there is nothing independent."[54] Christianity definitively introduced the principle of subjectivity into the world; God, the Absolute Idea, became human consciousness. Vischer reasoned: "Humor [the highest form of the comic] presupposes interiority; Interiority presupposes that consciousness view the whole world from a Christian perspective."[55] Moreover, this Christian perspective is one that has developed itself in history and is more complete in the contemporary German Christian spirit than it was in the past because the freedom and fearlessness of self-consciousness is a mark of modernity.

One reading of Hegel's philosophy, the reading of those whom Altenstein, the Prussian minister of education, admired, led to the conclusion that the principle of subjectivity introduced by Christ had been given substance in history and that the modern state and church, organic institutions embodying and manifesting the spirit, could be a "home" for the self and a context of its freedom. Vischer gave an alternate reading. The principle of subjectivity introduced by Christ was to be found in the German Christian spirit; but rather than find itself content and free within the institutions of the present, it manifested itself in a free criticism of them which began in the Enlightenment. The Enlightenment had not made its best contribution to art through the attempt of many of its representatives to judge and design art as a representation of "eternal, universal" moral principles.[56] It entered art legitimately in the irony of Friedrich Schlegel, and Hegel, at least a consistent Hegel, should not but have agreed.[57]

In Defense of Irony and the Criticism of Religion

It is likely that the censorship ban kept Strauss from being more explicit on *Wally the Skeptic.* He defended Gutzkow in the context of refuting Menzel's judgment on Goethe. The defense of Goethe's work, specifically, of its artistic right to depict moral confusion, a yearning for self-fulfillment, and a variety of subjects and aspects of experience is also a defense of *Wally* and of *The Life of Jesus* because Menzel had attacked all these works on the same grounds.[58] Of importance here is the shape of Strauss's defense and the correlation it makes between the defense of artistic rights and the right to theological critique.[59]

Strauss found Menzel engaged in an attempt to limit the German Protestant principle of spiritual freedom, which manifests itself in art as the depiction of a struggle to overcome any alienating dependency on external authority. Moreover, Menzel's demand that literature be supportive of "religion, morality, and the honor of the Fatherland" corresponded, in Strauss's opinion, to a demand for biblical literalism in religion.[60] The source of such demands was a misguided romanticism, the desire to recover a lost past. This past was "truly beautiful"; it was a time in which humans found themselves at home with a religion, a morality, and a political order, the truth of which to them was not subject to question. This ability to accept without question authority coming from outside the self was manifest, for example, in the early Christians (and also in "simple Christian people" of the present), who reasoned that because it was written, "Christ must have taught it."[61] Such an attitude corresponded with what could be called naive biblical literalism, an unquestioning acceptance of the factuality of the

Bible stories as they stand. Obviously, the theological rationalists had lost this naiveté, but so had the supernaturalists who took it upon themselves to argue against the rationalists. In other words, the very need to *defend* biblical literalism meant the loss of a time when the Bible's truth and stories simply corresponded with reality. Any attempt then to recapture the sure acceptance of the factuality of the Bible, including the Gospels, whether by tortured argumentation, as undertaken by committed Christian rationalists and supernaturalists alike, or by forceful assertion, could be seen as similar to the attempts of romantics and conservatives to recapture a lost political past.

"In a time of oppression," it could be a "political necessity" to try to revive a kind of faith which was capable of translating its own unquestioning acceptance into dedication to the "Fatherland."[62] But in the 1830s—as opposed to the times of oppression by the French prior to 1815—such a faith was out of place. The hope for the future, even for the political future of the Germans, did not lie in a return to the "simple, beautiful" past. Menzel's demand for a depiction of this return in art offered "only an anodyne, not a radical cure,"[63] for the insufficiencies of the present. The future could be brought in only by honesty and by giving free expression to the "spirit of the present."

This hopeful spirit of the present was the *critical spirit*, a spirit common to philosophers, historians, and poets. In denying poets their "rights," Menzel was in effect denying them their duty, the duty "to doubt and investigate."[64] The ground for this duty in the realm of art derived from the "task of poetry" itself, which was "to take its presentation from the world the way *it is*."[65] The form of realism that Strauss described here is an honest depiction in literature of the "mood of the times." It is not a presentation of the way things are in a descriptive fashion because "nothing is valued today merely because it exists."[66]

Hans Rosenberg quotes this statement of Strauss as exemplifying the mood of the young intellectuals of the 1830s. He comments: "The July Revolution had a decisive effect. After its occurrence, among the educated class, that is, among the academic youth, an unclear tendency toward absorption in empirical reality, a desire to go beyond established conditions, and an urgency for an effective contemporary expression [*Gestaltung*] predominated."[67] The "effective contemporary expression" identified by Strauss and Vischer as the expression of the mood of the times, the mood of *Wally*, was irony. They found the source for this formulation in the pre-Restoration heritage of the Enlightenment. In art, as in all other human expression, this ironic heritage of the Enlightenment grounded the rights of a subjectivity that had consumed "all objective determinations into itself" and was at present in the process of struggling to reappropriate the objective.[68] This struggle could not be ended by a "sterile" appeal to the old certainties, such as to the literal word of scripture. Such an appeal led to a false consciousness, a personal security possessed by those capable of embracing without question religion and morality as given realities but bought at the price of true humanity.

In describing "authentic" faith as doubt, Strauss came closest to a direct defense of *Wally the Skeptic*, in which Gutzkow had written that "the divinity is nowhere nearer than where a heart despairs of it."[69] But if "authentic" faith is this kind of doubt, where is the hope for the future of which Strauss wrote? Certainly he was not merely putting a stamp on a Schlegelian irony, which Hegel declared can become lost in yearning for the objective, for both he and Vischer maintained that irony is not the whole of art. True art, fulfilled art, moves beyond and through irony to the depiction of the unity of subjectivity and objectivity, to the unity of the ideal and the sensuous. Strauss directly criticized a literature that leaves only "negativity" and denies that any meaning or authentic human identity can be found in "human communities and institutions." Better authors depict "realistically and sympathetically" human struggle and moral confusion, but they also show or at least "hint" at a "rebirth of belief and morality."[70] This rebirth in both literature and life, however, can appear only in a new form, one which is adequate to a subjectivity grown free and strong.

For Strauss, as well as for Vischer, then, religion in its absolute form, Christianity, did not bring either the end of art or the resolution of the yearning produced by the irony of Greek comedy or the irony brought by the "mood" of the Enlightenment. Christianity, it seems, served to affirm the rights of that irony as the principle of spiritual freedom in art as in historical study. But if it affirmed those rights, then could it not also provide a ground for a move beyond "negativity?" Obviously, Strauss did not find the forms of Christianity around him in the 1830s—at least any that demanded a biblical literalism, in either a naive fundamental form or in the rationalist or supernaturalist form—adequate as this ground. His own challenge in *The Life of Jesus* to those forms of faith would be read by many of his contemporaries, as well as by subsequent interpreters, to be nothing more than a revival, if admittedly a powerfully composed one, of the Enlightenment's criticism of Christian belief. But to some of Strauss's contemporaries, his book not only represented a welcome revival of the Enlightenment as an assertion of what he and Vischer called "the rights of irony as the principle of spiritual freedom" but it also provided to them through its conception of Christianity more than anodyne and more than Schlegelian irony as well.

Irony and Beyond: The Narrative Structure of *The Life of Jesus*

Karl Ullmann (1793–1871), a disciple of Friedrich Schleiermacher and a friend of Vischer, was one of the few theologians of any persuasion to defend Strauss's "right" to depict doubt about the historicity of the New Testament narratives and even to bring that doubt to a "crisis."[71] Yet he accused Strauss of not showing "the positive power of the Spirit found in all true reformation theologians next to the critical and polemical elements."[72] This liberal theologian objected not so much to what Strauss had done in *The Life of Jesus* but rather to *how* Strauss had done it. Furthermore, he objected to what he called the "comic" mood of the historical study and to the fact that the announced subject of the study, Jesus, in his personality and deeds, fades into the background, giving up his place to the religious consciousness of his age. In these criticisms Ullmann sensed the element of *The Life of Jesus* that carried political meaning.

Ullmann termed comic that "lightness of mood," sometimes emerging as "biting satire," which characterized Strauss's relentless exposition of the flaws of the rationalists' and supernaturalists' attempts to explain the Gospels' historical reliability. To question the reliability of the gospel narratives of Jesus' life and even to bring about a crisis and demand a "sacrifice of ancient Christian beliefs" is the right of the historian and theologian; but the proper mood for such an endeavor, wrote Ullmann, is tragic. Strauss, on the contrary, took the most "dearly and deeply held Christian beliefs" and threw them "away as if they were soap bubbles."[73] Although he did not use the precise term, Ullmann had identified the comic irony in *The Life of Jesus.*

Many of the critics of *The Life of Jesus* denounced its tone or mood, identifying it as satirical. Ullmann himself noted and condemned the biting satire that sometimes appeared in the work. But the satirical passages, ones in which the stupidities of rationalist and supernaturalist interpretations are ridiculed, do not define the structure of the work, and they do not account for its political meaning. In fact, the emphasis on the satirical element in *The Life of Jesus* has obscured an understanding of its deeper ironic structure, which involved not merely an exposure or attack on foibles or vices but an inversion of what is taken as reality. In other words, exposure of error is part of the movement of *The Life of Jesus*, and sometimes this is done with ridicule, but it is the work's ironic inversion of what is considered reality that defined its overall structure and carries political meaning.

Comic irony is to be found in Strauss's investigations of the historicity of the narrated incidents in the gospel accounts of Jesus' life. In almost every case Strauss began his examination with a retelling or at least a recalling of what might be termed the common literal interpretation of these narratives. Next he relentlessly exposed the "flaws" in that interpretation, whether it be defended by rationalist or supernaturalist explanations, through exposing the absurdities implicit in those explanations. Finally, he showed that the way beyond these absurdities was to account for the text not as history but as myth, the product of the religious consciousness of Jesus' age.

The analysis of the scene at the baptism of Jesus by John provides a good example of his use of this technique. Strauss begins: "The synoptic Gospels tell us that at the moment John had completed his baptism of Jesus, the heavens were opened, the Holy Spirit descended on Jesus in the form of a dove, and a voice from heaven designated him the Son of God, in whom the Father was well pleased."[74] After bringing to mind this literal reading of the accounts of this event, stressing the sensory perception of it, he raises the question of how a cultured person who sought to reflect on this event could interpret it:

> First, that the visible heavens must divide in order for a divine being to appear on earth, that is, as if to descend from his accustomed seat cannot seem to have any objective reality. . . . Further, how is it reconcilable with the true idea of the Holy Spirit as the divine, all-pervading Power, that he should move from one place to another, like a finite being, and embody himself in the shape of a dove? Finally, that God should utter articulate tones in a national idiom has been justly held extravagant.[75]

Strauss proceeds to show how cultured minds, first supernaturalist theologians, and then naturalist, or rationalist, theologians, answered those questions.[76] Cultured supernaturalists tried to retain the divine origin of the event and its accounts, while modifying their apparent external absurdities. For example, one of them maintained that the crowd "saw and heard something" but that the vision of a dove and the voice of God were sensed only interiorly, not exteriorly. Strauss comments: "Our understanding fails us in this pneumatology . . . , wherein there are sensible realities transcending the senses and we hasten out of this misty atmosphere into the clearer one of those who simply tell us, that the appearance was an external incident, but one purely natural."[77] Natural interpretation said that Jesus and John, convinced of their identities, interpreted every happening in terms of their mission. This type of interpretation, when most consistent, retained the recorded happenings as actual, but it had difficulty accounting for how they *could* happen. Paulus was one who tried to do this, but in doing so, for example, "he had the hard job of showing through innumerable facts from natural history and other sources that a dove might be tame enough to fly toward man and how it could linger long enough so that it fit the description of abiding over Jesus."[78] After recalling the scene of the baptism as the evangelists relate it, Strauss leads the reader on to ask how long a well-trained dove could hover over someone's head. He does not leave his reader pondering this absurdity, however, but offers a more "intelligible" representation of the scene, explaining:

> In the east, and especially in Syria, the dove is considered to be a sacred bird. Because of its symbolism it was almost inevitably associated with the description of the Spirit moving on the face of the water given in *Genesis*. This symbolism was that of the enlivening warmth of nature and thus it perfectly represented the function which, in the Mosaic cosmogony, is ascribed to the Spirit of God,—the calling forth of creation. . . . Who then can wonder that in Hebrew writing the Spirit hovering over the primal waters is expressly compared to a dove, and that apart from the narrative under examination the dove is taken as a symbol of the Holy Spirit? How near to this lay the association of the hovering dove with the Messiah, on whom the dove-like Spirit was to descend.[79]

In essence, Strauss asks the reader: How can you not see that those who believed Jesus to be this promised Messiah would inevitably imagine a dove descending on him? In this case they embellished an event that probably actually happened, Jesus' baptism, with this central image of the Messiah from their religious heritage.

Beginning with the presentation of the apparently historical reality narrated by the text, Strauss moves through a "revelation" of the implicit absurdity of such a reading to a resolution that recognizes that what appeared to be historical is a product of human consciousness. Simply, the structure of the treatment of the recorded incidents in Jesus' life is *ironic*. In Hegelian language, self-consciousness, here the self-consciousness of the historical critic, beholds that "what had assumed the form of essentiality," here objective historical reality and givenness over against self-consciousness, "is instead dissolved within it."

Thus Strauss, as well as Gutzkow, used "irony as the principle of spiritual freedom." Both of them set self-consciousness over against "dearly and deeply held" certainties to expose the insubstantiality of those certainties. In Gutzkow's case, Wally exposes the insubstantiality of the social certainties and conventions of her day through her attempts, and consequent failures, to immerse herself in them. For Gutzkow's heroine, the exposure leads to despair and suicide. His novel ends with the negativity of an irony which, again in Hegel's terms, exposes "the nothingness of all that is objective." But as Ullmann saw, Strauss's *Life of Jesus* did not share in the tragic mood of Gutzkow's novel; its mode of irony was comic.

Strauss treated the loss of substantiality, the historical reality of the biblical narratives, with a sense of relief, or what he called a sense of "purgation," a feeling of freedom from the necessity of accepting as true what is in itself absurd.[80] But did this sense of "purgation" take one beyond the pitfalls that Hegel found in the irony of a Schlegel or of Greek comedy, in which self-consciousness is happy in thinking itself capable of maintaining the "bliss of self-enjoyment," but soon becomes a yearning for the lost substantiality?

To put this question another way, what in *The Life of Jesus* replaces the lost substantiality, the lost historical reliability of the texts and thus of the narrative incidents in Jesus' life? Certainly, it does not offer a scaled-down version of the historical life of Jesus or an "allegorizing" reinterpretation of the texts. Instead, time after time the text unmasks the activity of the religious consciousness of Jesus' age in the formation of the text. As a consequence, although Strauss did not deny that something, even Jesus' greatness of personality, *could* be known, whatever could be said of Jesus as a historical subject faded into the background, and the consciousness of the community replaced it as subject of the study.[81]

Ullmann objected to this loss of Jesus as subject in *The Life of Jesus*. Strauss's response to this objection revealed a potential in Hegelian philosophy for supporting something other than monarchy. He stated that in any historical development there is an interrelationship of causal forces—a both/and, and not an either/or. Great individuals like Jesus do create new communities, but they do so only when the times are right. At issue here is the question of the proper identification of the bearer and source of historical change, which, for the Hegelian, is also the bearer and source of meaning and truth in history. In what Strauss named the subjectivist view (in this context the one which would place Jesus in the foreground of a historical study of the Gospels), the bearers are individuals and their activities. In the objectivist view (here the one which would feature the consciousness of Jesus' age), the bearer is the ethos or collective consciousness of a people. From the Hegelian standpoint, neither view of history is complete by itself.[82] To support this assertion, Strauss used one of the planks of right-wing Hegelian Christology—Hegel's statement that "all actions, including world-historical actions, culminate with individuals as subjects giving actuality to the substantial." He pointed out that Hegel had gone on to say that these individuals are only fully understood as "the living instruments of what is in substance the deed of the world spirit," that is, not in their own uniqueness.[83]

In Strauss's opinion, the gospel narratives, "as written and received by believers," are clearly subjectivist history and, as such, unbalanced. They convey their religious theme, "the relationship of God to humanity," in a genre of history which Strauss named "holy" history or sagas (myth). This genre is characterized by a concentration on the personal, on "an inspired individual, such as a poet, a lawgiver, a prophet, or, in its highest potency, a God-man," to exhibit the relationship of God to humanity, rather than on the "objective," the depiction of this relationship "in an entire age, an entire people, in its natural interactions and mediation." Such a genre also stresses the suddenness and originality of that individual's achievements. Strauss said nothing here about the relationship of this genre to a particular age, but he also found elements of it in Plutarch's *Lives*.[84]

This discussion of the genre of the gospel narratives is illuminating because it has little to do, at least directly, with the post-Enlightenment, technically rationalist, difficulty of accepting miracle accounts as historical. Ullmann as a Schleiermacherian and Strauss agreed that the historicity of miracles was a difficulty. Thus, although miracles would be expected in this genre with its emphasis on "suddenness," it is the genre itself, not the miracles, which presents the problem. That problem is an excessive stress on the subjective to the extent that the individual depicted is atypical, divorced from his or her age. Faced with this subjectivist history, a good Hegelian must rewrite it to emphasize, admittedly also in one-sided fashion, the "objective," the ethos of Jesus' times, as also bearing meaning and truth.[85] The genre of the gospel narratives had to be changed in order to make clear that what was depicted there as belonging only to an outstanding individual belonged also to an entire people and, ultimately, to humanity itself. The featuring of myth, in the sense of the consciousness of the times, rather than the historical man Jesus accomplishes this change of genre.

The unmasking of the activity of the religious consciousness of Jesus' age, without the substitution of the "real" history of Jesus or an allegorizing reinterpretation of the texts, led beyond the illusory "happy consciousness" that follows comic irony but soon descends into the unhappy yearning for the substantial. In other words, the unmasking of the activity of collective consciousness as the subject of the study was itself the act of recovering the substantial.

Frei maintained that the German historians, in the tradition of Johann Gottfried Herder (1744–1803), who were concerned with the consciousness of an age as a subject for history moved toward a universalizing, spiritualizing view of history, rather than toward "realistic depiction," because the "historical subject-matter" in this perspective was "finally the one universal human spirit, even though always in specific cultural form."[86] Clearly, these remarks might seem to apply equally to *The Life of Jesus* and to identify it as an idealistic work abstracted from the concrete conditions of human life. As such, it would seem to have had little in common with the efforts of the Young Germans, who precisely sought to deal with such concrete conditions.

But *The Life of Jesus* and the founding work of the Young Germans, *Wally the Skeptic*, were immediately related to one another in the mid-1830s. The reason for this connecting is that they contained the same form of realism, the only form possible for expressing urgent social and political criticism in the Germany of that day. First, insofar as any definition of realism involves at least in some way the concept of the balance of subjectivity and objectivity, the alteration of the subjectivist genre of the gospel history through unmasking the collective consciousness of Jesus' age can be seen to be a move in the direction of those who desired to portray individuals' embeddedness in social and political conditions. It is an extreme move because *The Life of Jesus* does not merely reduce Jesus from a figure transcending his age to one conditioned by it but transforms this transcendent figure into the *product* of the age, albeit of the consciousness of the age. Second, when individuals in general are not agents in forming social and political conditions, as most were not in Germany, then realism understood as a representation of the balance of subjectivity and objectivity is, as Auerbach contended, not possible. If realism is taken also to mean a representation of the way things are, then only the past could provide material for it in Germany. Menzel understood this and urged imitation of the novels of Walter Scott. The Young Germans rejected Scott as a model, however, and turned to Balzac, whose novels Lukács described, in contrast to Scott's, as passing "from the portrayal of past history to the portrayal of the present as history."

The Life of Jesus moves in precisely this way. It passes from the presumably actual and normative history of Jesus through the collective consciousness of his age to the present. In other words, *The Life of Jesus*, in altering the Gospels' subjectivity, addressed contemporary readers who were locked in subjectivity, thwarted in their own religious development by their submission to an exhalted, outstanding individual of the past and thus lacking recognition of their own human potential as bearers of truth and meaning. That *The Life of Jesus* could raise Christian consciousness to a recognition of this potential and thus stir it as an agent of historical change did not escape those either on the left or on the right in Germany's politics. In fact, it can be said that the comic irony of *The Life of Jesus* was a more effective vehicle for conveying this recognition than was the tragic irony of *Wally the Skeptic*. And perhaps it came closer than the novel to providing that ideal opposition to existing institutions which Gutzkow said was the only realism possible for the radical, and thus to providing Germany with a genuine Aristophanian work.

In 1833, Heine wrote: "Most people think that with Goethe's death a new literary period began in Germany, that the old Germany went to its grave with him, that the aristocratic period of literature came to an end and the democratic period began, or as one French journalist expressed it recently, 'the spirit of man as an individual has ceased to exist, the spirit of collective man has begun.'"[87] Heine himself was not certain that he wanted to pass "judgement in such a categorical fashion on the future evolutions of the German mind."[88] In fact, he showed himself much more certain about the rights of poets to be skeptical than he was about what new kind of literature would succeed the Goethean Age. Yet if Heine had had Strauss's *Life of Jesus* before him in 1833, he might have found the French journalist's statement apropos of the future of German theology, if not of letters.

Arnold Ruge, who shared with Menzel and the Young Germans a concern with a politically effective literature, was to describe the 1835 edition of *The Life of Jesus* as "democratic." In reference to the role of myth as an expression of collective consciousness, Ruge judged that the work had accomplished a democratization of Christianity by making clear that the potentiality seeming to belong only to one exalted human belonged, rather, to humanity itself.[89]

The Young Germans, and many of the left-wing Hegelians, including Marx, had sought literary forms to express visions of a democratic society and to effect change. *The Life of Jesus* gave them such a form in theology. Although it concluded with what

Marx would denigrate as the idealistic terms of Hegelian philosophy, those terms, coupled with the entire structure of *The Life of Jesus*, made clear enough to some in 1835 that the text presented the "people," rather than the exalted, inspired individual, as the bearers of truth and meaning. This work inaugurated the "completed criticism of religion" in Germany announced by Marx not merely because it challenged the factual basis of Christianity; eighteenth-century rationalists and idealists had done that. Strauss's work was definitive because its historical critical endeavor was structured such that it captured "the spirit of the age." It presented an inversion in Christian theology that matched the inversion in literature and the corresponding inversion in politics desired by the Young Germans and other radical opponents of the Restoration.

In the Christian dogmatic conclusion of *The Life of Jesus*, this inversion replaces Jesus Christ as the God-man of Christian faith with the idea of the human species. By itself, this replacement could hardly have caused "panic-stricken terror" in Germany. For over a century, European intellectuals, including Germany's own Kant, had been offering the idea of Humanity as a proper modern substitute for the believer's Christ. Thus, when the conclusion of *The Life of Jesus* is isolated from the text as a whole, as it often is by those who use Strauss's intentions or theological tradition as guides to interpretation, it is impossible to understand how its restatement of what many radicals had come to despise as an empty ideal could inspire them and panic the conservatives. A divine human species sounds like the kind of safe *Biedermeier* and even philistine ideal which activists from Menzel to Marx sought to eliminate as prohibiting the recognition of the actual conditions in which men and women lived. But when read with the historical critical section and interpreted through its structure of comic irony, it becomes clear how this replacement of Christ by humanity carried the political meaning of radical democracy.

Chapter Four ❖ Christ and Democracy

Arnold Ruge was not alone in interpreting the Christ of *The Life of Jesus* of 1835 as an expression of the democratic principle. As Walter Jaeschke stated, "From the perspective of the philosophers of the Restoration, Strauss's *The Life of Jesus* destroyed the basis of the Christian monarchy."[1] The vehicle for this destruction was the "democratic" Christ, itself a product of an explicit interpretation of the categories of the most important German thought system of the day, a system supported by Education Minister Altenstein in the mid-1830s as the official philosophy of the Prussian government. Because *The Life of Jesus* combined a dramatic and popular expression of "the holy principle of spiritual freedom," an expression it had in common with *Wally the Skeptic*, with an affirmation of the truth of Hegelianism, it proved to have more power to disturb the Restoration German order than the novel. In other words, it introduced the principles of democracy as the consequence of its irony with more force than did *Wally the Skeptic* precisely because it claimed the strong tools of Hegel's philosophy.

Whereas *Wally the Skeptic* trailed off into what Menzel called "French" cynicism, *The Life of Jesus* engaged on its own ground the philosophy of the German Master. The potential effects of this difference are illustrated by the marked contrast between the conclusion of *Wally the Skeptic* and that of *The Life of Jesus*.

"French" Cynicism versus Hegelian Sublation

Caesar's "Confessions Concerning Religion and Christianity," sent as a letter to Wally, is the section of *Wally the Skeptic* that is least like *The Life of Jesus*. Certainly, there are some direct parallels between Caesar's "Confessions" and the academic life of Jesus. For one thing, Jesus is described in both as possessing apocalyptic illusions. Caesar saw him "as a young man . . . who, as a result of a serious confusion of his ideas, came to believe that his coming as the liberator of the nation to which he belonged had already been announced to his ancestors."[2] Furthermore, in both, the mythical nature of the New Testament narratives is affirmed. Caesar wrote that "later ages made an epic poem replete with miracles and a fabulous machinery of gods" out of the history of Jesus.[3] Finally, Caesar criticized, as did Strauss, the anthropomorphic God concept of the traditional revelation. He wrote, "To claim that all the writings were dictated by God means, in the dogma of inspiration, to make God party to all the solecisms and incorrect constructions that are to be found in the Greek text of the New Testament."[4] Indeed, the satirical tone sometimes used by Strauss and that used by Caesar in delineating the false ideas of biblical Christianity are similar.

Yet despite their agreement in these areas, Caesar and Strauss differed sharply on the meaning of their conclusions for Christian faith. In Caesar's opinion, "religion is despair over the purpose of the world,"[5] while to Strauss "religion is that form of the truth that is accessible to the people," truth in "popular guise."[6] Caesar judged that the Christian religion in history had not even proven itself to be the moral equivalent of the "dreamer Jesus"; Strauss, meanwhile, wrote that Christianity had developed with history to reveal its truth in ever more advanced stages of human consciousness. Caesar valued the historical Jesus over the symbolic Christ of Christian doctrine, finding it a "presumption [exceeding] the bounds of what is bearable [that] Christianity [has] its roots [not] in the teachings of Jesus"[7] but rather in a doctrine about his person as the God-man who died to save humans. Strauss, on the contrary, declared that when criticism destroyed the believers' historical Jesus, Christian faith lost nothing essential to itself because the seed of truth borne by the Christian religion was to be found precisely in the symbolic God-man.

The fundamental divergence between Caesar and Strauss was in their evaluations of Hegelian philosophy. Strauss defended it as the deepest philosophical truth which, although differing in form from Christian doctrine, was identical with it in content. In a sense, Caesar also found the truth content of Hegel's philosophy and Christianity to be identical, but he considered both to be relics of the past. He said: "Hegel's criteria everywhere is the past. His explanations are typical, his philosophy is an interpretation."[8] In the most searing judgment on Christianity of the "Confession," Caesar wrote:

> In short, Christianity is a religion that preaches the objective gospel of a human being. You poor rabbi of Nazareth! Instead of weeping over your dismal fate, they rejoice at your death and speak about it in laughing tones! The crucifixion of Jesus is not even historically felt anymore; instead, since everything in the unfortunate man's life is interpreted as being typical and necessary, sympathy and compassion cause one to pass indifferently over the pain and always to see on Good Friday only Easter, at the bed of a dying man a dreadful hand that pulls the pillow out from beneath his head in order that he may die faster, in order that he may arise faster! The crucifix has become an ornament that is hung from one's ear.[9]

In stark contrast, the young Hegelian Strauss wrote that a death and resurrection of the God-man is necessary to bring to humans the religious truth that God as Spirit goes out of himself into the finite, but returns to himself rather than losing himself. He explained: "The God-man, who during his life stood before his contemporaries as an individual distinct from them and perceptible by the senses, is by death taken out of their sight; he enters into their imagination and memory: the unity of the individual human in him becomes part of the general consciousness; and the church must repeat spiritually, in the souls of its members, those events of his life which he experiences externally."[10]

As much as any in *Wally the Skeptic*, Gutzkow's passage about the rabbi of Nazareth approached his aesthetic goal of producing a work of social realism, a work that would "insure that no one who lived in a glistening palace in the middle of a ghetto where the poor have nothing but ragged cloth to cover them has a quiet night."[11] But as was typical with his work, description gave way to musings of consciousness, and, in this case, Caesar made explicit what was conveyed in these startling images: "Christianity seems to get in the way of political emancipation everywhere."[12] In another passage which could well have been a commentary on the young pastor Strauss's assertion in Klein-Ingersheim that it was better for his farmer congregation "to perish from lack of earthly bread than suffer from a lack of heavenly manna, the word of God,"[13] Caesar gave qualified approval of the French social philosophers Saint-Simon (1760–1825) and Lammenais (1782–1854) because they avoided "the effrontery that directs starving workers toward the heavenly bread of eternal life." He continued, "The religion of renunciation may be fitting in years where the harvest has not been sufficient; but where Plenty and Waste celebrate their festivities all around, mankind grumbles at a religion that appeals always to submission, humility, the counsel of God."[14]

Caesar's cynicism about Christianity and its corresponding cultural expression in Germany, Hegel's philosophy, is unrelieved. Under the influence of this cynicism, Wally declines in spirit and commits suicide. Perhaps Caesar was predicting this end when he wrote to her, in an obvious allusion to Hegel, that "the healthy portion of humanity will be swept along by another current of the stormy world spirit."[15] The world spirit is a villain who destroyed the rabbi of Nazareth and Wally.

The action of this world spirit also provided the ending to *The Life of Jesus*. It was a happy, comic ending. Hegel's philosophy of Absolute Spirit offered the believer truth in the form of philosophical concepts to replace truth in its common religious form, a tangible historical Jesus, which had been apparently destroyed by the action of historical criticism.

The conclusion of *The Life of Jesus* identified the truth of the Christian doctrine not with a suffering rabbi, Gutzkow's symbol for actual suffering humanity, but with the truth of a German cultural product that some sought to appropriate to support Restoration politics, specifically the Prussian government and aristocratic privilege. Perhaps the crucifix that Gutzkow described as an earring was intended to call to mind one being worn at the court in Berlin. To identify the truth of Christianity with the Hegelian Idea then, as *The Life of Jesus* did as its final consequence, would at first seem to be far removed from Gutzkow's effort, however marred, to introduce a social realism into German culture, and thereby instigate political changes in the direction of democracy. But because *The Life of Jesus* linked what it had in common with *Wally the Skeptic*, the bold exercise of irony, the "holy freedom" to doubt and test the given, to the realization of the identity of the truth of Christian doctrine and the Hegelian philosophy, it produced a startling theological consequence. Its revelation that the *true* identity of the God-man of Christianity was the human species presented a more serious challenge to the Restoration Christian monarchy than did the dead Wally. A Christ who was depicted in the language of Germany's most eminent philosophy to be what Heine had referred to as "the spirit of collective man," rather than the "spirit of man as an individual," was far more threatening to the political order than the image of a young woman destroyed by the disease of *Biedermeier* culture.

The first step toward understanding why the comic ending of *The Life of Jesus* posed such an effective political threat is to trace in some detail the movement of its Hegelian conclusion. In it, the ironic pattern of the historical investigation of the story of Jesus is repeated. Initially, an apparently integral "speculative" Christology is presented in a capsule version of the Hegelian philosophy of religion. Next an unresolved dilemma about the Christ as the unity of divinity and humanity emerges and presses forward the question of his identity. Finally, resolution comes in the form of the revelation of the true, comprehensible identity of the Christ.

Strauss began by showing how the reality of the God-man is necessitated by the Hegelian idea of God. An apparently whole and satisfying Christology is laid out. He wrote,

> When it is said of God that he is spirit, and of man that he is also spirit, it follows that the two are not essentially distinct. It is the essential characteristic of spirit to remain identical with itself in the distinction of itself from itself, that is, to possess itself in others. Thus, to speak more precisely, it is given with the recognition of God as spirit that God does not remain as a fixed and immutable infinite outside and

above the finite but rather enters into it, posits finitude, nature and human spirit merely as his alienation of self from which he eternally returns again into unity with himself. As man, considered as a finite spirit, limited to his finite nature, has not truth; so God, considered exclusively as an infinite spirit, shut up in his infinitude, has not reality. The infinite spirit is real only when it discloses itself in finite spirits; as the finite spirit is true only when it merges itself in the infinite. The true and real existence of spirit, therefore, is neither in God by himself, nor in man by himself, but in the God-man; neither in the infinite alone, nor in the finite alone, but in the interchange of impartation and withdrawal between the two, which on the part of God is revelation, on the part of man religion.[16]

This truth of God must be made evident to humans as "a certainty for the senses," "a human individual who is recognized as the visible God."[17] Moreover, this God-man must die to "prove that the incarnation of God is real, that the infinite spirit does not scorn to descend into the lowest depths of the finite."[18] But the God-man must also rise to prove spirit's return to itself out of its alienation and to render the unity of the divine and human nature "part of the general consciousness," part of the consciousness of every believer.[19]

The most sophisticated and comprehensive rationality of the 1830s thus seemed to verify the orthodox doctrine of the God-man and even to give grounds for deducing the validity of gospel history from philosophy. But did it? One central and glaring dilemma appeared. "The general propositions on the unity of the divine and human natures do not in the least serve to explain the appearance of a person in whom this unity existed individually in an exclusive manner."[20] The basic problem is granting all the power of the subduing of nature found in Hegel's conception of God as spirit to a single man to exercise through "individual, voluntary acts" or identifying the triumph of spirit over mere natural life with "the bodily resurrection of an individual."[21] Such an empowered individual and body are inconceivable, unreal, merely fantastic. The Hegelian philosophy with its assertion that the rational is actual cannot suppress the question: "If reality is ascribed to the idea of the unity of the divine and human natures, is this equivalent to the admission that this unity must actually have been once manifested, as it never had been, and never more will be, in one individual?"[22] The Hegelian philosophy cannot suppress this question about the identity of the God-man.

In the final stage of his Hegelian conclusion, Strauss unmasks the true Christ—the idea of the human species. The idea of the species is the proper "subject of the predicates which the Church assigns to Christ."[23] Humanity, not an exclusive individual, can receive the power of spirit. Humanity can be a miracle worker "in so far as in the course of human history the spirit more and more subjugates nature, both within and around man, until it lies before him as the inert matter on which he exercises his active power."[24] Moreover, humanity can be said to rise from death because "from the suppression of its mortality as a personal, national, and earthly spirit arises its union with the infinite spirit of the heavens."[25] Appealing to Luther's preference for Christ's spiritual miracles over his physical miracles, Strauss asks the reader how he or she could possibly not want to see the true identity of Christ: "Shall we interest ourselves more in the cure of some sick people in Galilee, than in the miracles of intellectual and moral life belonging to the history of the world?"[26] In effect, he asks why one should not see collective humanity as the miracle worker and agent of the life-enhancing world spirit. Ruge gave the answer that to see this would be to see the truth of the democratic principle, to see a democratic Christ.

To explicate how the conclusion of *The Life of Jesus* interpreted the Hegelian philosophy as supportive of the democratic principle entails following a historical debate about the meaning of the Hegelian category of subjectivity in the social model of life, which replaces the rationalist mathematical model as the one capable of grounding true reason and thus an adequate logic. Some of the systematic significance of the category of subjectivity was laid out in the first chapter. A deeper journey into Hegel's system is not the route which will enable us to follow the historical debate about subjectivity. Its conditions were set often by clearly inept philosophers, including Menzel and some of the Hegelians themselves. Certainly,

Strauss, by contrast, excelled as an agile thinker who was conversant with a wide range of Hegel's works. Moreover, the political meaning of the conclusion of *The Life of Jesus* is bound together with its clear success as an interpretation of Hegelianism. Nevertheless, this meaning cannot be discovered by assessing the "correctness" of this interpretation according to an inner consistency found in the Hegelian system or attributed to it according to Hegel's intent. The political meaning is found through the route of the historical reactions to the text.

As a more accurate guidepost along this route, Strauss's own reading of the Hegelianism of *The Life of Jesus*, undertaken during the heat of the trial of the text, will be used. A major element in this defense is his response to the charges, which were hurled at him by Berlin Hegelians, that his text did *not* represent Hegel's position. The specialized content of this directly Hegelian part of Strauss's defense of *The Life of Jesus*, which intellectual historians continue to debate on the grounds of its "true" or "false" Hegelianism, becomes useful as a guide to the interpretation of the political meaning of the text only when it is related to Strauss's overall defensive tactic on Hegelianism. This is a tactic of taking upon himself the defense *of* Hegel against the charge of his being an establishment philosopher. Even in the specialized Hegelian part of his total defense, Strauss did not set out to prove directly his own Hegelian orthodoxy. Instead, he put his accusers alongside Menzel as representing Hegel as an apologist of the status quo. In Caesar's terms, the Hegel put on trial is the one whose "criteria everywhere is the past," whose "philosophy is an interpretation," whose world spirit is a villain. Strauss's tactic is to vindicate Hegel as a philosopher whose world spirit is rather a hero who allows for the freedom of comic irony and who would save, rather than sweep away, Wally by changing the oppressive conditions of her times.

Before narrowing the focus to interpret the conclusion of *The Life of Jesus* with the help of Strauss's retrospective reading, the politically significant reactions to the text must be examined. These reactions, which set the conditions of the historical debate and the charges against Strauss, show how the seemingly esoteric language of Hegelianism was readily translated into everyday political language.

Christ and Monarch

In 1837, Karl Bretschneider, who in 1835 published a defense of rationalism's own political respectability, *Theology and Revolution*, wrote a review of *The Life of Jesus*. In it he concluded, as had many others, that the book confirmed the dangerous political nature of Hegelianism, a system he named "philosophical idolatry."[27] Bretschneider found in Hegelianism the same tendency that Heine had found analogous to French democracy in the "religion of Germany's greatest thinkers," pantheism—"to divinize the life of man in not only its spiritual, but also its material side."[28] He placed Hegelianism in the same category as the radical philosophies of the author of *Lucinde*, Friedrich Schlegel, of the Young Germans, and of the Saint-Simonians!

The Life of Jesus assured that Hegelianism would be suspected of a hidden affinity with the stances of such figures; many, such as Menzel and Hengstenberg, immediately associated *The Life of Jesus* with the works of social and political radicals. It is no wonder then that Bretschneider, a rationalist, saw in *The Life of Jesus* an occasion on which to join forces even with those who sought to make a disjunction between rationalism and an ecclesiastical supernaturalism that corresponded with government from above.

The tendency of Hegel's philosophy to undermine such a disjunction had been criticized before the appearance of *The Life of Jesus* by philosophers of the Restoration, who held that the existence of a personal God was the sole basis for a genuine state and questioned the political implications of Hegel's potentially pantheist concept of God as Absolute Spirit.[29] Using the axiom "Personality is the magic of unity, which no change destroys," Julius Stahl had argued that only self-consciousness could provide the unity and completeness necessary to all change and limit and thus a personal God was the necessary guarantor of the unity and laws of the state.[30] Only a "free subject, a personal God," could provide unity to the state. And he maintained that the manner in which this divine unity of the state could be actualized was the monarchy.[31]

By the early 1830s, Stahl's polemic against pantheism had extended itself to an onslaught on Hegel's philosophy of Absolute Spirit, which he understood as denying a personal God. At that time, however, his charges had little effect because the Hegelians in Berlin were able to maintain their position as defenders of Protestant orthodoxy. Moreover, personality as essential to the unity of the state and as grounding the necessity of a monarch was also an element of Hegel's discussion of sovereignty in *The Philosophy of Right*. There he wrote:

> Sovereignty, at first simply the universal *thought* of [the ethical] ideality [of the state], comes into existence only as subjectivity sure of itself, as the will's abstract and to that extent ungrounded self-determination in which the finality of the decision is rooted. This is the strictly individual aspect of the state, and in virtue of this alone is the state *one. The truth of subjectivity, however, is attained only in the subject and the truth of personality only in a person*; and in a constitution which has become mature as a realization of rationality each of the true moments of the concept [universality, particularity, and individuality] has its explicitly actual and separate formation. Hence this absolutely decisive moment of the whole is not individuality in general, but a single individual, the monarch.[32]

Around 1843, Marx would assert that *The Philosophy of Right* was not a description of an ideal state but rather a veiled description of the real (oppressive) Prussian state of Hegel's day which sought to justify it with "mystical" language. He commented on Hegel's definition of sovereignty: "Thus, because subjectivity is actual only as subject, and the subject only as one, the personality of the state is actual only as one person. A beautiful conclusion. Hegel could just as well conclude that because the individual man is one the human species is only a single man."[33]

In 1835, *The Life of Jesus* showed, in effect, that Hegel could not possibly be so "mystical" or irrational. *The Life of Jesus* had concluded with the assertion that Absolute Personality, the

Absolute Spirit, could not be actual only as *one* person; rather divine subjectivity was only truly actualized in the human species. In other words, it declared untenable in the sphere of religion that which Hegel seemed to be saying was tenable in the sphere of the state. The crucial theological question asked was precisely: "If reality is ascribed to the idea of the unity of the divine and human natures, is this equivalent to the admission that this unity must actually have been once manifested, as it never had been, and never will be, in *one* individual? This is indeed not the mode in which Idea realizes itself; it is not wont to lavish all its fullness on one exemplar and be niggardly toward all others."[34] This answer was made clearer: "[As the] key to the whole of Christology, that as subject of the predicate which the Church assigns to Christ, we place, instead of an individual, an idea; but an idea which has an existence in reality, not in the mind only, like that of Kant. In an individual Godman, the properties and functions which the Church ascribes to Christ contradict themselves; in the idea of the species, they perfectly agree. Humanity is the union of the two natures—God become man."[35]

In October 1837, Altenstein sent a copy of Bretschneider's review of *The Life of Jesus* to Karl Friedrich Göschel (1784–1862), the epitome of right-wing Hegelianism.[36] Altenstein urged Göschel to defend the religious orthodoxy of the Hegelian system in the face of the threat posed to its reputation by *The Life of Jesus*, and Göschel produced a response in order to "cut Strauss off of the Hegelian stem."[37] In order to do this, he "made explicit the political implications of the [Christological] model conceived of [and expressed] by Strauss apolitically."[38] Furthermore, he drew direct parallels between the monarch and Christ, the state and the human species, and consequently between the relationships of the monarch to the state and Christ to the human species. Not only for a Hegelian, for whom all parts of a systematic philosophy are interrelated, but also for anyone attuned to the philosophies of restoration even in their popular form, Göschel's associations would have made sense.

The theologian argued from *The Philosophy of Right*, specifically from the necessity of a hereditary monarch to the actualization of the sovereignty of the state, to establish the orthodoxy of Hegelian philosophy of religion: that is, its support of the necessity of the *one* man, Christ, as the God-man. As Jaeschke points out, Göschel virtually argues that Hegel *did* intend to say what Marx accused him of meaning—"to represent the monarch as the actual God-man."[39] Thus at issue is the parallel between an interpretation of Hegel's *Philosophy of Right* on the question whether subjectivity as the unitive principle of the state must be realized in one man, the monarch, and Hegelian theology's interpretation of the question whether subjectivity as the principle guaranteeing the concrete unity of God and humans must be realized in one man, Christ.

The inter-Hegelian discussion prompted by *The Life of Jesus* about the meaning of the principle of subjectivity was at base then a discussion about the nature of God as person, a vital topic at a time when the personality of God was considered to be an essential support of the Restoration monarchy. Göschel merely made explicit what others did not—the necessity of the model of monarchy to a right-wing Hegelian theological understanding of this principle.

In his defense of the hereditary monarchy in *The Philosophy of Right*, Hegel wrote: "This ultimate self in which the will of the state is concentrated is, when thus taken in abstraction, a single self and therefore is *immediate* individuality. Hence its natural character is implied in its very conception. The monarch, therefore, is essentially characterized as *this* individual, in abstraction from all his other characteristics, and *this* individual is raised to the dignity of monarchy in an immediate, natural fashion, i.e., through his birth in the course of nature."[40] Göschel used this assertion that the hereditary monarch as immediate individuality, *this* person, as a single self, can be identified with the subjectivity of the state to ground the orthodox claim that the one man Christ could be identified with the subjectivity of substance, with God. His arguments made evident how the conclusion of *The Life of Jesus* on the historical truth, as well as the philosophical necessity, of a single God-man was immediately taken as an attack on the historical truth and philosophical necessity of a single embodiment of the state in a monarch, indeed, in a Christian monarch, as the earthly representative of the personal God.

As a tactic, Göschel began by agreeing with Strauss that "the whole of humanity, the human species is Christ," but he parted with Strauss by accusing him of not knowing that the full realization of the Hegelian idea is reached only at another stage of reason, the stage where it is realized that "the species itself is a person, that the collectivity is a unity."[41] The collectivity, in the state as in the species, cannot attain personality, cannot by itself reach the concept of *person*, because essential to this concept are individuality and subjectivity, which are actual only in *one* individual not in the whole. In other words, collectivity does not have an *actual* personality, only a "mystical or ideal personality."

In this argumentation, Göschel was appealing to the statement in *The Philosophy of Right* that "personality, like subjectivity in general, as infinitely self-related, has its truth (to be precise, its most elementary immediate truth) only in a person, in a subject existing 'for' himself, and what exists 'for itself' is just simply a unity. It is only as a person, the monarch, that the personality of the state is actual. . . . A so-called 'artificial person,' be it a society, a community, or a family, however inherently concrete it may be, contains personality only abstractly, as one moment of itself."[42] Göschel concluded that just as the state achieves actual personality in the monarch, the human species achieves it when a head—an individual, namely, Christ as a single person—is given to it. This head is "an *Urmensch*," a real, autonomous individual actualizing personality and providing the conditions of possibility of personality for all humans, singly and collectively.[43] Humans achieve personality as individuals to the extent that they allow "themselves to be penetrated by this single individual [Christ] as the monarch of humanity."[44]

Here is the pattern for the right-wing theological Hegelianism that would stress the assertion that the principle of subjectivity was introduced to the world by Christianity in the God-man and that would support an orthodox interpretation of the

Incarnation from statements made in defense of the monarchy in *The Philosophy of Right*, of which the (Christian) principle of subjectivity forms the basis. The right-wing Hegelians and Göschel drew a direct parallel between the monarch and the God-man.[45] *The Life of Jesus* was read as an argument against the drawing of that parallel and thus against a motif central to restoration philosophy as well as to orthodox Hegelian theology. Most significantly, it was read as a relapse to Enlightenment rationalism, which meant politically a relapse to the principles of the French Revolution.

The question that divided the theological Hegelians and Strauss was not only whether Hegel's God and Christ were orthodox but also whether Hegel's model of self-consciousness, of subjectivity of substance as Absolute Truth, eliminated all vestiges of the principles of analogy found in common rationalism, *Verstand*.[46] Did it result in the extreme of subordinating human thought to what is given to it? Did it serve simply to justify the given in theology and, as Marx and Menzel charged, in politics?

As a statement of Hegelianism, *The Life of Jesus* answered no to these questions. Jaeschke declared correctly that *The Life of Jesus* appeared in the context of the 1830s "as a rebirth of rationalism modified by Hegel's philosophy"; thus it unveiled "the affinity between rationalism and idealistic speculation" which had been hidden.[47] *The Life of Jesus* offered itself as an interpretation of Hegel's philosophy in which the function of *Verstand* was given a necessary role in the realization of the religious ideal, the actualization of the truth of Christianity. On the grounds of this role, it unveiled the potential within Hegelian philosophy to be the philosophy of revolution, not restoration.

Restoration or Progress

In his defense of *The Life of Jesus*, Strauss vindicated Hegel's concept of God against Menzel's charges that it served to justify the given and thus to support restoration. Central to the interchange between these men, now brother journalists, was precisely the question of how Hegel's social model of life as self-consciousness was related to Schelling's biological model of life as nature.

The south German liberal Menzel fought Hegelianism with the same vigor that he mustered against Gutzkow's destructive "French" radicalism, and indeed he associated the Berlin philosopher with the political journalist even before Strauss's *Life of Jesus* verified the link so dramatically. But he accused "French" radicalism and Prussian reaction as equally destructive of true German progress. In criticizing Gutzkow's Jesus as portrayed in *Wally the Skeptic* as a "simpleton," he declared that it had been influenced by the philosophy of Hegel because in that philosophy God is said to have attained only a dim consciousness of self in Christ, one revealed merely in representations (*Vorstellungen*), whereas God is said to come to *clear* consciousness first in philosophy and really only in the philosopher Hegel's mind![48] In fact, anticipating Marx's criticism, he declared that Hegel's mind, in possession of the principle "All that is, is rational," simply served to show "that the present condition is the most rational, and that it is not only revolutionary, but . . . unphilosophical to take any exceptions to it."[49]

In contrast to this idealism in support of the status quo, Menzel placed the "progressive" philosophical system of Schelling. He termed the system epical and compared it to the politically progressive historical novels of Walter Scott because, like those novels, Schelling's philosophy achieved a balance between interiority and exteriority, described here as the rights of reason and historical rights, a balance which was necessary to truly German freedom. Thus Menzel extended the criteria of his form of realism in literature directly to philosophy. Failing to achieve a balance between the admittedly characteristic reflective nature of the German people and external action to change history was the common flaw of Gutzkow, the novelist, and Hegel, the philosopher. Schelling's philosophy, on the contrary, "endeavors to secure to every spiritual existence, be it a character, an opinion, or an event, the same right in a natural philosophy of mind and history which it does to every material existence in common science. . . . According to this system, there is a growth and progress, a multiplicity and an order, in the intellectual world, as in the natural one."[50]

As a German loyalist schooled in the anti-French sentiment in the wars of liberation, Menzel shared with Hegel the rejection of French rationalism as cold, destructive mechanism, and he sought a unique German freedom that was in continuity with the peculiar traditions of his homeland. But he thought that Schelling's philosophy, not Hegel's, achieved the balance of subjectivity and objectivity, the balance of the rights of reason and the rights of history, necessary to German freedom. He understood Schelling's as an organic philosophy extended analogically from nature to history understood as permeated by laws of regularity. Progress, or change, was thus grounded in the laws of growth embedded in history, and those laws functioned analogously to those in biological nature. Sympathetic to the model of biological life and its capacity to account for the uniqueness of German development, Menzel, as a liberal, stressed the principles of analogy as part of the model. But he understood that cut off from analogy, the model could support merely historical rights, that is, a philosophy of restoration.

In light of the political contention between the rights of reason and historical rights, and distinguishing a subjective "pole," correlate with reason, from an objective "pole," correlate with history, Menzel judged that Schelling's disciples had carried his balance of subjective freedom and objective historical realization too far to the objective side, giving history all the rights. In opposition, "Hegel made the subjective pole again the center," as had Johann Gottlieb Ficthe (1762–1814). But Ficthe's subjectivism, although not achieving balance with objectivity, at least promoted "a noble, vigorous me, willing only the good." Menzel wrote: "[In contrast] Hegel's center was a mere thinking, petty, conceited self-satisfied *little me*, speculating on the hearth. Knowing well what would better suit the temper of the times, he carried back Ficthe's beautiful effervescence to a cold, heartless arrogance; his enthusiastic fullness of youth to a prematurely crafty, aristocratic hollowness; and became the philosopher of the restoration, as Ficthe had been the philosopher of the revolution."[51]

Menzel went so far as to accuse Hegel's disciples of identifying the Master's mind itself with God: that is, of carrying subjective Idealism to an absurd extreme. Relying particularly on an analysis of Hegel's *Logic*, he declared Hegel's philosophy to be nothing other than a simple inversion of Schelling's philosophy of nature into a philosophy of self-consciousness, of Schelling's identification of nature and God into the identification of the "I," indeed Hegel's own "I," and God, which was then used to justify Restoration government, specifically that of Hegel's employer, the Prussian government.

Just as Menzel had condemned Gutzkow and Hegel on the same grounds, Strauss defended them on the same grounds. Admitting that both stressed reflectiveness, the freedom of self-consciousness, he insisted that nevertheless both the novelist and the philosopher addressed themselves to the real world, in fact, to changing the real world, and did not, as Menzel charged, retreat into the joys and illusions of an egotistical interiority. Ruge praised this explanation of the meaning of Hegel's God as Absolute Spirit as both timely and correct.[52]

Strauss charged that Menzel had failed to see that "the identity of subject and object, which Schelling merely postulated as an intellectual intuition, was deduced and explicated in [Hegel's] *Phenomenology* and *Logic*."[53] Hegel's philosophy was no mere mystification, no deification of mind; it accounted for and grappled with the objective world rising only through a stringent series of mediations to the identity of subject and object. Strauss admitted that in a certain sense the form of the categories and concepts developed in Hegel's *Logic* was abstracted from the diverse forms of life in nature and history. But this "indifference of form" signified neither a lack of differentiation between the self-consciousness of the human knower and God as the Absolute nor the dissolution of nature and history into mind, as Menzel had asserted. Strauss mused sarcastically that Menzel might be able to understand Hegel's own description of his *Logic* because that description sounds mystical: "[The *Logic*] develops the essence of God, as it is before the creation of nature and a finite spirit."[54] But as the totality of Hegel's system shows, that primordial essence of God is realized in all the realms of nature and finite spirit. If Menzel had had any capacity to understand Hegel, he would have seen that the *Logic* demonstrates that it is in the essence of God to be so realized.

Strauss argued that because of his refusal to follow the rigors of true thought, Menzel wallowed in "mystical," romantic blindness, and thus had interpreted in an immanentist direction Hegel's famous statement from his *Encyclopedia*: "Without the world God is not God (in the full sense); God is himself, only in so far as he knows himself; his self-knowing, moreover, is his self-consciousness in humanity."[55] Menzel had read it to mean that man is the substantial, God only the accidental—that is, merely present in the consciousness of humanity. Since he had not been able to follow Hegel's own explication of the sense in which subject and object are unified, he could not see that this assertion is descriptive of God's own essence, not of human mind, and certainly not of Hegel's individual mind as primordial, as Menzel had asserted in his more obtuse moments. God, for Hegel, is the primordial, the Absolute. His statement describes God's essence as Absolute Spirit, and it means: "God, in order to be conscious of himself, renounces himself, posits the world opposite himself; this world rises from the deepest point of God's renunciation, unconscious nature, to humans, in whose God-consciousness the divine essence is mirrored."[56] Thus Hegel's description of the unity of human spirit and Absolute Spirit does not mean that humans are prior to God or equal to God, nor does it mean that they are absorbed into God. Humans are rather a "station in the cycle of divine life," that place where "God returns to himself from his renunciation in nature, where God unites with himself."[57]

Menzel's major failure, which Strauss attributed to his leanings toward mysticism, was his inability to comprehend Hegel's many assertions about the nature of the identity of God and humans, of finite spirit and Absolute Spirit. Because he focused exclusively on the statements describing that identity as a "distinctionless unity," while ignoring the equally prevalent descriptions of that identity as "essentially the unity of distinctions," he showed no grasp of Hegel's all-important notion of "concrete unity." The Hegelian "concrete unity" of God and humans is one in which the integrity of its two sides is retained. With its syllogism of Spirit, Nature, and Idea, Hegel's *Logic* was precisely an attempt to provide the terms in which to understand the unity of finitude and infinitude as "concrete": that is, as capable of including real difference and thus relation and mediation between the sides. It did not collapse the terms to one side, as did the "abstract" concepts of unity in the Kantian or Spinozan systems.[58]

Strauss maintained that a philosophy such as Schelling's which merely asserts the unity of the infinite with the finite by way of intuiting the infinite in nature results in a vision of sameness, of "eternal rest," in which a divine self-identity is repeated over and over again in time. Such a system contains par excellence the principle of *stability*. In contrast, Hegel's system of mediation can account for change and progress because it allows for real difference between God and the finite and yet understands that difference as overcome in the process of God advancing through stages to self-realization. In short, Strauss held that a "pantheist" philosophy, such as that which Menzel admired in Schelling, supports the status quo, while Hegel's promotes progress. Strauss made this clear in his defense of the Hegelian statement "All that is, is rational" as an antistability principle. Strauss wrote of Menzel: "Does not the Barbarian know that in Hegel's system there is a great difference between being [*Seiendem*], merely existing [*Existirendem*] and being actual [*Wirklichem*]?—that Hegel in no way calls all that is present as such actual?—that the actual for Hegel is only the most essential kernel of being surrounded by an extensive shell of mere appearance?"[59] Because Hegel's famous sentence, if read correctly, "sanctions as rational *only the essential* in what is present at any given time," it is clearly opposed to any principle of stability.[60] This statement affirms the same view that Strauss expressed in his defense of irony, in which he wrote that nothing is valued merely because it exists.

Strauss added political proofs to this corrected reading of Hegel's theoretical statement. He declared that if Menzel had read Hegel's discussion of the Würtemberg Assembly of 1815 and 1816, he would have recognized that "our [south German] liberals had to go to schools to [Hegel] to learn what liberalism is."[61] The reference here is to a brief essay in which Hegel criticized the Würtemberg Diet, which in the eighteenth century had been compared to England's Parliament, for becoming a defender of aristocratic privilege. In describing this essay, Jürgen Habermas has said that in it "Hegel asserts the rational validity of abstract bourgeois law against the accidental historical character of the traditional rights of the freedom of the estates. Thus philosophically he deploys the world-historical results of the French Revolution against those whose understanding of themselves lags patriarchially and uncomprehendingly behind the concept of the modern state."[62] In this text, Hegel wrote:

> The picture of a better and juster time has become lively in the souls of men, and a longing, a sighing for purer and freer conditions has moved all hearts and set them at variance with the actuality [of the present]. . . . General and deep is the feeling that the fabric of the state in its present condition is untenable. . . .
>
> How blind they are who may hope that institutions, constitutions, laws which no longer correspond to human manner, needs, and opinions, from which the spirit has flown, can subsist any longer; or that forms in which intellect and feeling now take no interest are powerful enough to be any longer the bond of a nation![63]

Strauss did not stop at calling to mind Hegel's apparently more liberal past. He noted a similar critique of given conditions in *The Philosophy of Right*, which he stated firmly did not sanction the Prussian system of government, as Menzel said it did. In contrast to what existed in the Prussian system of the 1830s, Hegel espoused, for example, "trial by jury, a two house parliament system, and public debates among estates."[64] The corporations, which for Hegel constituted "the fundamental support of life in the state," had been passed over in the Prussian state.[65] In other words, Prussia did not actualize

Hegel's theory that organizations, "circles of association in civil society" that were even without any action of the state already communities, were what mediated between the state and an undifferentiated—that is, atomized—civil society.

In *The Philosophy of Right*, Hegel wrote: "The circles of association in civil society are already communities. To picture these communities as once more breaking up into a mere conglomeration of individuals as soon as they enter the field of politics, i.e., the field of the highest concrete universality, is *eo ipso* to hold civil and political life apart from one another and as it were to hang the latter in the air, because its basis could then only be the abstract individuality of caprice and opinion."[66] Such a theory of organizations within civil society as bearing within themselves the unity necessary to the cohesiveness of the state obviously could conflict with the restoration political theory of the absolute necessity of a monarch as the source of unity for any state. Strauss did not hide this conflict. On the contrary, he drew the ready conclusion by stating that it was consistent with Hegel's political philosophy that "the power of the sovereign [be confined] within far more narrow boundaries than [had] been done in Prussia."[67]

The differences between Hegel's ideal state and the Prussian state are merely listed by Strauss with no elaboration, but it is clear that the point of the list is that Hegel's philosophy supported representative government, and thus more freedoms for individuals than the Prussian state allowed. In this context, his mention of Hegel's theory of the corporation is directed against a theory of a monarchial state which attempted to repress constitutionalism and representative assembly. Since it is not a defense of "democracy" in its more restrictive political meaning of a "one person, one vote" political system, it puts Hegel in the camp of German liberalism, and not in the camp of French radicalism. The implicit politics of *The Life of Jesus*, and not Strauss's direct defense of Hegel against Menzel, would accomplish the moving of Hegel to the more extreme left, and a more "German" form of sovereignty by the people.

In this defense, however, Strauss highlighted a crucial element of Hegel's *Philosophy of Right* to which Ruge and others found *The Life of Jesus* directly related. This element is the question whether civil society has within itself the capacity to be political. In Hegel, civil society is defined as the sphere of private interest and individual rights, while the political state is defended as the sphere of universal law. The issue is how civil society and political life can be unified. Hegel held that the failure of the French Revolution and its ideal of radical democracy as the means for achieving this unity stemmed from the French inability to conceive of the state as an organism. He drew an analogy between the results of common rationalism in thought and the Terror which followed the Revolution, comparing their passions for mathematical equalization and their consequent inability to conceive of qualitative difference.[68] Only abstract individual right could be supported in this model; thus the only means of effecting a political unity was death, a negation of individuality that was inevitably locked into singleness and separateness. True reason can provide an organic concept of the state capable of unifying without destroying the individuals of civil society; according to Göschel, a hereditary monarch was essential to this unifying power. What Strauss stressed to Menzel was that some aspects of Hegel's *Philosophy of Right* seemed to place unifying powers within civil society itself, thus lessening at least the prominence of the role of the monarch, of the *one* person as the essential source of unity.

In *The Life of Jesus* the defiance of the monarchy is far more extreme. There, not just certain circles of associations among individual humans but the human species itself are asserted to possess the power of unity. This is why the one man, Christ, is not needed. Hegel's replacement of traditional logic's syllogism, whose members are the particular, the individual, and the universal, with a syllogism whose members are Nature, Spirit, and Idea is used to support this assertion. In Hegel's *Logic*, the Idea is said to be, on the fundamental level, the idea of life, and this idea is given "a reality that is itself [abstract] universality" in the species.[69] In *The Life of Jesus* the Hegelian idea of life is introduced not as an idea of biological life, and thus as abstract, but as an idea of social life, as the idea of the *human* species. Strauss wrote that the way to overcome the contradiction between the properties that the church had ascribed to Christ is to understand that "in the idea of the species, they perfectly agree."[70] It is to understand that "humanity is the union of the two natures—God becoming man, the infinite manifesting itself in the finite, and the finite spirit remembering its infinitude; [the idea of the species] is the child of the visible Mother and the invisible Father, Nature and Spirit.[71]

But what keeps this idea from being a merely abstract universality like Kant's idea of humanity or like the merely numerically infinite idea of humanity which showed its murderous potential in the French Revolution? How can this idea replace the one individual, manifest as Christ and as the monarch, which the Hegelian Göschel claimed necessary to the *unity* of humanity and the state? The idea of the species is concrete in *The Life of Jesus* because it is a social, fully related idea; it is the very power of social relatedness as it works itself out in history. Humanity is the miracle worker, transforming physical nature *and* human nature. In other words, the content of this idea of humanity is historical humanity creating its own nature by creating culture. As Strauss wrote, "Now the main element of that idea is that the negation of the merely natural and sensual life, which is itself the negation of spirit, is the sole way to true spiritual life." Humanity accomplishes this negation in working its miracles of self-development, in transforming and transcending physical and biological life, even the limits of "personal, national and world spirit."[72]

In the "German Ideology," Marx gave what can serve as a succinct answer to the question of why the idea of the species in *The Life of Jesus* is not abstract. He wrote, "But the essence of man is no abstraction inhering in each single individual. In its actuality it is the ensemble of social relations."[73]

It is easy to understand how, when Göschel's parallels are applied to the conclusion of *The Life of Jesus*, it can be said that in substituting the human species for the God-man it substituted a model of popular sovereignty for the monarchy. Humans, collectively, are the bearers of the subjectivity of substance and thus they are the subjects of history. But even this sort of assertion about humanity's potential would not have had the effect it did if it had not been the conclusion of a historical investigation, that is, if it had not been linked to a critical examination, rather than an interpretation, of the past.

Rationalism within Hegelianism

In his direct response to the charges made by fellow Hegelians that in *The Life of Jesus* he had fallen away from Hegel's philosophical standpoint, Strauss admitted that they were to some extent correct when they cried out that his book did not express their position:

> Indeed, it is not their meaning. They live in the good faith that, *when they have established an idea in a gospel account, its historical truth is thereby demonstrated.* And when they appeal to Hegel himself and assure us that he would not have recognized my book as an expression of his meaning, they say nothing against my own conviction. Hegel was no personal friend of historical criticism. It annoyed him, as it annoyed Goethe, to see the heroic figures of antiquity, on which they lovingly hung their great opinions, gnawed at by critical doubt. Meanwhile, if these were cloud-puffs which they took to be rock formations, they did not want to be made aware of it; they did not want to be disturbed in the illusion by which they felt exalted.[74]

Nevertheless, if Hegel had been true to his own logic, he would have had to affirm historical criticism just as he would have had to affirm Schlegel's irony as necessary to the attainment of Absolute Truth. Moreover, the theological Hegelians' attempts to prove the necessity of the historical validity of all or part of the gospel literature from the necessity of the idea was, according to Strauss, a blatant departure from the logic of Hegel's system. He did not use the phrase "inversion of the subject into the object" later used by Marx to describe the tactic by which "an empirical existent is taken in an uncritical way to be the real Truth of the Idea,"[75] but in effect he described the "inversion" of what he understood to be the proper dynamic of that system by the theological Hegelians as doing just that.

Certainly, the theological Hegelians had recognized Hegel's critique of Kant's abstract reason, for they used it, although unjustly in Strauss's opinion, against him. But in their desire to assert the unity of the rational and the real over against the Kantian standpoint, they, not he, were the ones who had fallen behind Hegel, in this instance, to the standpoint of Schelling—of pantheism. Like Menzel, these Hegelians had forgotten that for Hegel the true grasp of the Absolute, of the Absolute which comprehends the finite, the determined, the individual, and does not dissolve or destroy it, proceeds from no mere assertion or intuition of the Absolute. The true grasp of the Absolute is reached only by a series of mediations, and as Strauss stated to Menzel, it is Hegel's *Phenomenology* and *Logic* which mark his advance beyond Schelling.[76]

The crux of Strauss's argumentation is that if there is a place for the critique of consciousness in philosophical knowing, there must be a place for it in theological knowing. If for Hegel there is a philosophical dialectics, there must also be a theological dialectics. In philosophical knowing, sense certainty, the immediate grasp of the given, is only the first moment in the rise to truth. Similarly, in theological knowing, the certainty of belief, the immediate grasp by religious consciousness of the object of belief, "dogma or sacred history," can only be the first moment in the rise of truth. Furthermore, "the progress from this beginning point in theology can be none other than in philosophy, that is, a *negative* mediation, by which that beginning point becomes a subordinate one, which is not for itself the true."[77] When the Hegelian theologians attempt to relate this theological beginning point, the immediate grasp of sacred history, in a solely affirmative manner to the end point, the truth of the idea of the Incarnation, they deny "*The Phenomenology* in the whole territory of religion." But to deny the *Phenomenology* is to fall back into Schelling's "night in which all cows are black": it is to fail to recognize the inadequacy of the form of the finite to *immediately* bear the contents of the Absolute and thus to fail to preserve the finite as finite.[78] It is to fail to recognize interrelatedness.

The fully consistent theological parallel to Schelling's philosophical attempt to grasp the Absolute immediately in intuition is the attempt to assert that the immediately given is the Absolute, or what is the same, "to give philosophy in its relation to the Christian religion the task of conceiving the biblical, namely gospel, facts as facts."[79] Strauss maintains that to do this is to do in the field of theology what Julius Stahl does in the field of political philosophy![80]

In theology to use the Idea in this way results in the failure to recognize the inadequacy of the *form* of that which is believed to immediately bear the contents of the truth of the Idea of the Incarnation. Hegel's distinction between religious representation (*Vorstellung*) and philosophical concept (*Begriff*) was the key to the promised peace between Christianity and modern thought. But theological Hegelians in Berlin betrayed the Master's promise with their treatment of biblical history. They attempted as if by holding a mirror in front of us "to lead us up above the fact to the idea only to guide us back again from the idea to the fact as such."[81] Nothing moved, and thus the distinction between representation and concept was rendered meaningless. Something had to happen in the transition from representation to concept. It was historical criticism which could help it happen because it, and it alone, could clarify what Hegel had left ambiguous in the realm of theology, that is, the relationship between gospel history and the philosophical concept.[82] Hegel was clear in asserting that the content of religious representation and philosophical concept is the same, while the forms of representation and concept are different. But where did he place the facticity of the gospel narratives? If he placed it on the side of the content, it would indeed be given together with the truth of the Idea. If he placed it on the side of the form, however, it would be incidental to the truth of the Idea, and thus historical criticism would be freed of any philosophical or theological constraints.[83]

In contrast to Schelling and Spinoza, Hegel claimed to have

attained a conception of unity which retained distinction. Strauss maintained that this was possible because his speculative standpoint superseded but did not destroy the standpoint of common rationalism. He argued that in the theological equivalent to Schelling's philosophy, that which is believed would be established to be the truth "by a kind of *clairvoyance*."[84] There would be no movement of "stepping outside and over" what is given in believing certainty and thus no means of distinguishing between content and inadequate form.[85] Historical criticism is that which "steps outside and over" and "distinguishes" in theology. Moreover, it has for its "sole presupposition . . . the similarity of all happenings."[86] Historical criticism functions like common rationalism: that is, as that which separates, distinguishes, and determines by means of universal law, similarity.[87] Just as it is the action of common rationalism which sets the philosophical dialectic in motion in the *Phenomenology*, it is historical criticism which sets the theological dialectic in motion.

Historical criticism functions in theology to distinguish the elements in what is grasped in believing certainty, the religious representation. Believing certainty receives the gospel stories as they appear, that is, as though they were fact. What it receives is the *apparent* history of the individual Jesus as the God-man. By separating what is indeed fact from what only appears to be fact, historical criticism functions as common rationalism functions in the philosophical process, that is, to identify the finite, the determined as the finite and determined. The role of historical criticism is not to destroy the finite, the determined, the individual—not to dissolve it into the infinite, as did Spinoza, or to justify the murder of the individual, as Hegel claimed it did in the French Terror—but rather to dispel the *immediacy* of the identification of Jesus with God, given to believing certainty in the Gospels, because that immediate identification, *if it remains unaltered*, is itself what destroys all possibility of real difference. Believing certainty is lacking "if it is arrested at the common this, this miracle, this person, this piece cut off from the rest of history and reality."[88]

It is only after the *negative* mediation, performed by historical criticism in demonstrating the determinateness, the finiteness of Jesus, that the truly *affirmative* theological dialectic can begin. As in philosophical knowing, it is only after the clarification of determinateness by common rationalism that the dialectical process is moved to overreach determinateness in rising to the true Absolute. In the theological dialectic, it is only after the determinateness of Jesus is recognized for what it is that "the here and now of this event," God's becoming man, overreaches itself into another here and now "until it is recognized as a universal event."[89]

The invocation of Hegel's statements of the subjectivity of substance did not solve the dilemma facing Hegelian theology: "If reality is ascribed to the Idea of the unity of the divine and human natures, is this equivalent to the admission that this unity must actually have been manifested, as it never had been and indeed never more will be, in one individual?"[90] Is the affirmation of the actual existence in history of the God-man of orthodox belief essential to the Hegelian affirmation of the subjectivity of substance? *The Life of Jesus* answered no; Christian belief is lacking if it is arrested at "the common this," *this* person, cut off from the rest of history and reality. It is lacking if it does not see Christ as the power of interrelation in human life.

Altenstein and Göschel saw political trouble ahead for theological Hegelians if this conclusion stood. It could be read to affirm that the modern state was also lacking if it was arrested at "this person." Hegel had written that "the monarch, therefore, is essentially characterized as *this* individual, in abstraction from all his other characteristics, and *this* individual is raised to the dignity of monarchy in an immediate, natural fashion, i.e., through his birth in the course of nature.[91] It was dangerous to suggest that his philosophy did not consistently support this assertion. In effect *The Life of Jesus* substituted the sovereignty of the people for the sovereignty of the monarch. Marx would claim that without the *mystification of inversion* Hegel's political philosophy did indeed affirm this sovereignty of the people, did affirm that the vehicle for realizing the subjectivity in the state is the subjects themselves. Marx wrote:

> Had Hegel started with the real subjects as the bases of the state it would not have been necessary for him to let the state become subjectivified in a mystical way. "However, the truth of subjectivity," says Hegel, "is attained only in a subject, and the truth of personality only in a person." This too is a mystification. Subjectivity is a characteristic of subjects and personality is a characteristic of the person. Instead of considering them to be predicates of their subjects Hegel makes the predicates independent and then lets them be subsequently and mysteriously converted into their subjects.
>
> The existence of the predicate is the subject; thus the subject is the existence of subjectivity, etc. Hegel makes the predicates, the object, independent, but independent as separated from their real independence, their subject. . . . This is the dualism: Hegel does not consider the universal to be the actual essence of the actual, finite thing, i.e., the existing determinate thing.[92]

The Life of Jesus declared that "that which is rational [*Vernünftige*] is also real [*wirklich*]; the idea is not merely the moral imperative of Kant [*ein Sollen*], but also actuality [*ein Sein*]."[93] But it asserted that to be actual, the subject and the predicate of the rational and real had to agree.

The correct solution to Christology is found by making the subject and predicate of the church's dogma of the Incarnation agree, or, as Marx put it, to see that the existence of the predicate is the subject. "Humanity is the union of the two natures—God become man."[94] Instead of remaining with irrational belief in a single God-man, *The Life of Jesus*, by exercising the right of common rationalism, unmasks the real subject of Christian faith, the consciousness of the early Christian community, and then ultimately the human species itself. It declares that there is no need to "mystify" Christianity and find its subject in *one* individual.

Marx wrote: "What kind of ideality of the state would it have to be which, instead of being the actual self-consciousness of the citizens and the communal soul of the state, were *one* person, *one* subject[?] . . . What is important to Hegel is representing the monarch as the actual 'God-man', the actual incarnation of the Idea. . . . [But the] predicate, the essence, never exhausts the sphere of its existence in a single one but in many ones. . . . [Not one man but rather] democracy is the truth of monarchy."[95]

Göschel, Altenstein, and many others heard anticipations of these bold sentences in *The Life of Jesus*; they recognized the political implications of the conclusion of the theology book—not one man but rather democracy is the truth of Christianity.

God as the World Historical Hero

While it is true that the Hegelianism of *The Life of Jesus* rendered it ultimately a more potent instrument of political protest than *Wally the Skeptic*, the literary qualities of *The Life of Jesus* that associated it immediately with the works of the Young Germans are the fundamental reason for its power. In other words, even in the atmosphere of the 1830s an interpretation of the philosophy of Hegel in a theologically unorthodox manner could have been put on the shelf if it had not so dramatically and skillfully evoked the radical spirit of the day. If the technical Hegelian conclusion had not been preceded by the acting out of the unmasking of Jesus Christ, *The Life of Jesus* would have been no more powerful than many other idealistic works. There can be no doubt that, used in defense of *The Life of Jesus*, Strauss's polemical pen made it difficult for the right-wing Hegelians cavalierly to dismiss *The Life of Jesus* as a "pantheist" misreading of Hegel. But if Strauss moved with ease through the Hegelian system to demonstrate how neither Hegel nor *The Life of Jesus* was pantheist, the whole drama of the text served to prove that both were in a sense just that.

In 1834, Heine had lauded the potentially revolutionary God of what he called German pantheism, and it is that God which the drama of *The Life of Jesus* placed center stage in 1835. Heine wrote:

> [God] manifests himself most magnificently in man, who both feels and thinks, who is able to distinguish himself as an individual from objective nature and already possesses in his intellect the ideas that pre-

sent themselves to him in the world of phenomena. In man the deity attains self-awareness and reveals this self-awareness again through man. This process does not take place in and through the *individual* human being, but in and through *collective* humanity, the result being that every human being comprehends and represents only one portion of the divine universe, whereas collective humanity will comprehend and represent the totality of the divine universe in idea and reality.[96]

Thus Heine too explained why humanity does not need *one* man, as Christ or monarch, to give it unity. Humanity has the ability to be a unity as part of its essence because "God is therefore the real *hero* of universal history, which is his never ending thought, his never ending action, his word, his deed; and we can rightly say of all mankind that it is an incarnation of God."[97] It is wrong, said the poet, to think that this kind of religion, which he without a qualm called "Pantheism," leads humans to political indifference.

The God of *The Life of Jesus* is the God of what Heine called modern German religion, which he held was given its form by the Reformation. This God, while keeping the role of actor in history depicted in the Bible, does not act supernaturally on the world as did the personal biblical God. Rather, this God frees humanity from any pseudodivine finite restraints on its self-realization. Heine held that the characteristic form of religion in Protestant Germany in the 1830s was far removed from the form of religion in Catholic France in the 1780s. Pantheism, "the religion of Germany's greatest thinkers," was not like French Catholicism. Instead it was like French materialism, because it tended to the physical conditions of human existence, "the material happiness of the peoples." Thus, at base, German pantheists were natural allies of the French materialists, who had resorted to political revolution to bring about the betterment of material conditions for all humans. The only difference between the two systems was that the German pantheists were motivated not by hatred of the spirit, as was the French materialist, but by their belief in the incarnation of God's spirit and their desire to foster the life of the spirit.[98]

In the language of the master of German Idealism, *The Life of*

Jesus expressed the democratic principle as the genuine Protestant Christian meaning of belief in the Spirit. In a sense, because it insisted on testing the claims of Christian dogma, indeed of the Hegelian system, by empirical criteria, it demonstrated the affinities that Heine found between French materialism and German Idealism. This demonstration held more potential to stir political sentiments than Gutzkow's anti-Hegelian "poor rabbi of Nazareth" or religiously doubtful Wally. As a sort of culminating expression of the religion of Germany's greatest thinkers, *The Life of Jesus* might have had the potential to galvanize Protestant Christians to revolutionize German society, as the French had done theirs. Clearly, the book threatened the advocates of the Restoration, and for a time it did pull together a political left, but it did not inspire a successful democratic revolution. Part of this failure can be attributed to the alteration of *The Life of Jesus* in the third edition. This edition, which Ruge named aristocratic, severely damaged the symbolic status of the text for the left because it clearly abandoned the democratic Christ. An analysis of this aristocratic third edition can help make the political meaning of the first edition even more evident, as well as explain why that meaning was not espoused by German Protestantism in the Pre-March.

Chapter Five ❖ Aristocracy and Genius

Even as late as 1842 the Prussian government was demanding that the members of Young Germany sign a promise not to write anything threatening to the government, morality, or religion. By this time, however, many of the Young Germans had earned the scorn of those on the political left for turning "the universal into the subjective, reality into literature, and life into ideology," as well as for remaining abstract and flighty.[1] The left-wing Hegelian Arnold Ruge was among those who accused the members of Young Germany of these sins, and in 1843, while all of them except the stubborn Gutzkow signed the promise and made peace with Prussian censorship, Ruge's *Halle Yearbooks* were banned. During the Pre-March era, those who were on one day revered spokespersons for political freedom were often the next day accused of the crimes of "subjectivism" and "idealism" by disillusioned followers. The left-wing Hegelians accused even Hegel of these crimes, and their symbol of freedom, Strauss, drew those same charges soon after he had led the disciples of Hegel to the left in 1835.

The ground for their accusation was the third edition of *The Life of Jesus*, published in 1838. Strauss significantly altered *The Life of Jesus* in the third edition. He also issued two companion pieces, "What Is Transient and Permanent in Christianity" and "Justinus Kerner," collected under the telling title *Two Peaceful Letters* (1839).[2] This altered life of Jesus and its peaceful apology did not win Strauss approval from his theological associates. To his orthodox Pietist opponents, the 1838 *Life* was no more acceptable than the first edition. More liberal theologians, such as the followers of Schleiermacher, to whom it might have been expected to appeal, rejected the work as too tentative.[3] To those who were on the *political* left, like Ruge, Strauss's third edition of *The Life of Jesus* was no more acceptable than it was to theologians. The history of Ruge's expression of disdain for the book gives striking evidence of the fluidity of the positions of those desiring freedom from Restoration government in the latter half of the 1830s. One of Strauss's *Two Peaceful Letters*, "Justinus Kerner," was solicited by Ruge to be the lead article in the very first issue, 1 January 1838, of the *Halle Yearbooks*. Although the third edition of *The Life of Jesus* was substantially finished by then, it was not printed until April 1838. By May 1839, in Ruge's response to this edition, which he included in his review of *Two Peaceful Letters*,[4] he had judged Strauss capable of supplying comfort to reactionaries.[5] He named the third edition "aristocratic," identifying it with the heritage of Romanticism and the revival of Pietism.

In the third edition, Strauss gave as the official reason for the revision of the first edition his changed opinion about the historical accuracy of John's Gospel.[6] Although the historical accuracy of the synoptic Gospels had been questioned by many scholars of the early nineteenth century, only Karl Bretschneider, the articulate defender of theological rationalism, had questioned the historicity of John. In fact, John's Gospel had been the mainstay of liberal theology, providing the blueprint for its image of Jesus as the historical person who possessed the fullness of human perfection. The most famous expression of this image of Jesus was found in the Christology of Schleiermacher, who held that Jesus possessed absolute perfection of God-consciousness: that is, an awareness of God's creative activity that dominated every moment and thus every expression and action of his life.[7] In his own lectures on the life of Jesus, Schleiermacher compared Jesus to a creative artist, which he defined as one who is guided in the artistic activity by his or her unique impulses or inner images rather than by some sort of extrinsic model, whether ideal or real.[8] Schleiermacher's Jesus thus bore affinities to the creative "genius," a concept used by German Classicists as well as Romantics and one still alive in the 1830s.

This type of Jesus not only had cultural relevance in early-nineteenth-century Germany but also seemed to the "cultured" believers to be defensible on historical grounds. For example, in his lectures on the life of Jesus, Schleiermacher held that although the accuracy of the sayings of Jesus in the synoptic Gospels could be questioned, the Gospel of John was that of an eyewitness, and its discourses provided the biblical scholar an access to the interiority or intentionality of Jesus. From this point of view, it was possible to contend, as indeed Strauss himself did in his third edition, that even if the external events related in the Gospels could not be verified as historically accurate, because the discourses reported in John's Gospel were authentic or at least close approximations of Jesus' words, knowledge of the personality and the actual, historical man Jesus was attainable through historical investigation.

In the conclusion of the third edition, Strauss described the Jesus who could be known as a result of his revised historical investigations. He wrote:

> Jesus belongs to the category of highly gifted individuals who in the various spheres of life are called to raise the development of Spirit in humanity to higher levels. These are individuals whom in fields outside of religion, namely those of art and science, we are accustomed to call geniuses. To be sure, Christ is not hereby once again introduced into the properly Christian sanctuary, but first only into the Chapel of Alexander Severus [the Roman Emperor who was a religious syncretist], where he stands next to Orpheus and Homer, not only next to Moses but also to Muhammed—indeed where he dare not scorn the company of Alexander and Caesar, of Raphael and Mozart. . . . Therefore, by putting aside the concept of sinlessness and absolute perfection as unattainable, we conceive Christ as the one in whose self-consciousness the unity of the divine and human first appeared with sufficient energy to reduce to *a disappearing minimum* all the hindrances of this unity in the whole range of his soul and life. He is the one who to this extent remains unique and unequaled in world history, without, however, having to deprive the religious consciousness first achieved by him of purification and further development in details through the progressive formation of the human spirit.[9]

Thus, in contrast to the first edition of *The Life of Jesus*, the third edition focused on the subjectivity of Jesus. If publically Strauss explained that he changed this edition because he had become unsure of his previous objection to accepting the authenticity of the Gospel of John, privately he talked about a failure of nerve. He wrote to Vischer that he had learned that *Teufel*, the devil, rhymes with *Zweifel*, doubt: "When one passes through the first phase of doubt into the second phase, doubt about doubt begins. The second doubt does not cancel the first doubt and return one to belief or certainty. Instead it produces pure confusion and vertigo in which one loses all literal sense."[10] He assured Vischer that the "return to belief" in question was not "religious belief" but "purely scientific." Vischer responded to his friend in a direct and somewhat harsh manner, saying, in effect, "Do not fool yourself—you do not question your scientific principles. You feel lonely and isolated." He compared Strauss to a hero in a tragedy who, when surrounded by his enemies, becomes partially wrong in his own "pathos" in becoming "mellow and weak."[11]

Whatever Strauss's intentions in writing the third edition, the aesthetician Vischer's term, pathos, is an apt one for describing its characteristic principle. It is not correct to say that this edition was of a different genre from the first. Rather it introduced alien elements into the structure of the first edition which destroyed its unity, and these are elements of pathos in the sense that they are emotional or subjective elements, in contrast to the universal or objective element, the ethos. In the first edition, the objective element, the religious consciousness of a group, predominated. In the third edition, a subjective element, the individual personality of Jesus, was introjected. The mythical consciousness of first-century Palestine gives way to the individual hero, Jesus. In short, a genius steps stage front. As a result of this change of focus, the cutting edge of the first edition's comic irony is lost and the shock of the dissolution of beloved scenes in the narrated life of Jesus is blunted. As will be seen, it is precisely the transformation of comic irony into pathos, into what he most often calls a cult of genius, that the Hegelian Ruge identifies as the reactionary aspect of the third edition of *The Life of Jesus*.

Strauss interpreted his initial life of Jesus through the Hegelian view of history, which he maintained comprehended both a subjective and an objective side, both the actions of great individuals and of collective forces. The duty of the truly Hegelian historian was to be responsive to the needs of the present time and to insure the proper balance of the subjective and the objective by stressing whichever side the times were lacking. In 1835, Strauss considered that to be the objective side, but he did concede to the Schleiermacherian Ullmann that historical investigation of the Gospels could reach a subjective side, some knowledge of the greatness of Jesus' personality. In the 1838 edition, this subjective side comes to the fore. Apparently joining the theological Hegelians by now deleting the second half of Hegel's famous description of the world-historical individual, Strauss explained in the third edition,

> Indeed, only when scientific Christology has passed beyond Jesus as a person will it be forced to turn back to a consideration of him again and again. "All actions, including world-historical actions, culminate with individuals as subjects giving actuality to the substantial." Generally speaking, the various directions in which the wealth of the divine life is set forth in humanity (e.g., in art and science) are represented by great individuals. Especially in the field of religion, at least within the domain of monotheism, all new epochs and characteristic formations are attached to a prominent personality. Should Christianity alone be made an exception to this rule? Should the most forceful spiritual creation be without a demonstrable founder, simply the result of the collision of scattered powers and causes?[12]

The obvious question for the Young Hegelians who had admired the original *Life of Jesus* was whether such an emergence of the subjective was right for the times.

The extreme of a subjective side of history was to be found in *genius*: that is, in the manifestation of spontaneous creativity coming from inner impulses. Here an individual adds something new to the culture that does not seem to be derived from the culture at all. Thus, this type of creative subjectivity possesses inward freedom, internal resources that transcend the external limits of cultural forms. As we saw in Vischer's description of irony as the holy principle of spiritual freedom, this type of inwardness in art and religion could be a force for reform because it fostered a rebellion against the restrictions of outworn forms. But inwardness in art and religion could also "turn into a force against reform"; it could attempt "to maintain the purity of the self at the expense of relating to the world."[13] Ruge, for example, saw Pietists in the 1830s as reactionary in contrast to the Pietist followers of the genuine reformer Jacob Spener (1635–1705) in the seventeenth century. To him, the modern Pietist was "a product of the enervating emotional letdown of the peace following the War of Liberation [who] thus manifests the culture's loss of confidence and inward self-doubt after the strenuous, manly deeds of war."[14] Because this modern type of Pietism lacked the energy of Spener's type, it found itself, as in the person of Hengstenberg, at home with the very hardened orthodoxy that the seventeenth-century Pietist fought.

To Ruge, a Hegelian, the antidote for reactionary inwardness or subjectivity was self-conscious reflection. Because it comprehended the Absolute Spirit as universal truth realizing itself through finite forms, speculative thought insured a role for collective forces in history when an ideal of inwardness lost contact with the world. For those who like Ruge believed in the progressive potential of Hegel's philosophy, "reflection alone completed the freeing that feeling [or interiority] only begins."[15] Later, of course, the belief in the freeing power of thought would be derided by ex-Hegelians like Marx as ineffective and even escapist idealism; but in the latter half of the 1830s, the battle among those young intellectuals who sought political freedom centered on realizable ideals and what role subjective and objective forms of human consciousness played in making ideals actual.

In the framework of this disputed Hegelian theory, then, inwardness, spontaneous and free feeling, genius—all elements of the force of creativity—found truth only in being balanced by genuine objectivity, that is, not merely by externality but by speculative thought as a collective force. The issue at hand was which one German culture in the 1830s needed to give it the balance necessary for it to "lead humanity to a unity with itself that is also in concert with the objective world."[16]

In order to understand why Ruge decided that the religious model of a genius Jesus was not at all what Germany needed, some common associations between the concept of genius and political stances in the 1830s need to be examined.

Genius and the New Religion

In "Transient and Permanent Elements in Christianity," Strauss described the popularity of cults of genius in the mid-1830s. He wrote: "At present, monuments for great men, for noble spirits, rise up everywhere out of an impulse which has spread like a miasma throughout Germany. There is much that is comic about this trend, but it has its serious side and it is a sign of the times."[17]

Statues were not the only form in which the popularity of the cult of genius was evidenced. In 1834, a young woman, Charlotte Stieglitz, created a sensation in Germany by committing a sacrificial suicide. Her husband was a struggling, unsuccessful poet, and she, convinced of his talent, sought to arouse his genius by providing him with the soul-wrenching emotions that she believed inspired creative acts. Her husband remained mediocre in his poetry, but Charlotte became an instant legend, inspiring more talented writers. Gutzkow wrote, "Whoever would possess the genius of Goethe and could endure the fact that people would speak of imitation, could in telling the story of Charlotte write an immortal companion piece to *Werther*."[18]

The Young German, who more than likely took inspiration from Charlotte's death himself in the writing of *Wally the Skeptic*, linked her death with the July Revolution, repressive academic and social education, new French social philosophy, and the influence of Bettina von Arnim (1785–1859), the eulogist for Goethe, as an "example of the lightning . . . that was bound to ignite the sultry atmosphere of Germany."[19] He was apparently not alone in his association of the symbolic act of Charlotte and the potential for disruption of German peace and quiet. Hengstenberg first attacked the 1835 edition of Strauss's *Life of Jesus* in a place where, as Kramer has pointed out, "one would hardly expect to find such a criticism," as a sidelight of his literary review of the book *Charlotte Stieglitz: A Memorial*, written by another Young German, Theodor Mundt.[20]

In fact, Hengstenberg campaigned against the upsurge of the cult of genius not only as it formed around the memory of Charlotte but also in the shape of the popular "worship of the Weimar Olympian," Goethe. In this he saw a new religion which could threaten Christianity and the political order. In a style that approximated Heine's, Strauss described the new religion arising in Germany. He declared that the German people had forgotten how to build churches. They either wanted to erect their own large halls or they "mimicked childishly, like the frog mimics the bull, the ancient cathedrals." However, since they did not have the creative energy to build new halls, they instead erected statues for the Germans they considered great. Strauss agreed with Hengstenberg that this trend was a new *form* of religion, but he did not see it as incompatible with Christianity. He wrote:

> A new paganism, or perhaps just as well said, a new Catholicism, has arrived over Protestant Germany. One incarnation of God is now not sufficient, and there has arisen a desire for a series of ever more complete Avatars such as are found in Indian religion. Around Jesus, who used to stand alone, the people want to put a garland of other holy persons; only now these are not merely the holy people that the Church has named, but as in the chapel of Alexander Severus, next to the statues of Christ and Abraham, that of Orpheus was found. This is a mark of the time, to venerate the Spirit of God in all the spirits, who have affected humanity in a vital and creative way.[21]

Indicative of the convictions of the age, this tendency evidenced what Heine had called the secret religion of Germany's greatest thinkers, pantheism—the belief that the authentic revelation of God and God's true incarnation takes place in the whole of humanity and that no one individual has a special claim qualitatively to embody the divine differently from any other individual. Strauss traced the beginnings of this pantheism of the 1830s to the response to those writers, such as Kant, who declared nature devoid of the divine by those who, like Schelling, wrote of the apotheosis of God in nature. In more recent times, the newest philosophy, Hegel's, had "learned to see the self-revelation of the divine essence" not only in nature but also in the world of the "spirit in art, the state, and history."[22]

Even Menzel believed in divinity as the nourishing soil of history. He, Strauss, and Heine all described an attitude common to their cultured contemporaries that human life is the locus of divine activity and thus that human life is itself worthy of veneration. However, exactly what form that veneration should take—the imitation and worship of artistic creativity, the adulation of historical heroes, or dedication to the transformation of the conditions of society out of respect for the divine presence in everyone's life—was an unsettled issue.

In his query about the fate of the epigonal generation, Heine described the ambiguity of the worship of cultural heroes on the occasion of the death of Goethe:

> It is as if in this year Death suddenly became an *aristocrat*, as if he wanted to distinguish particularly the notables of this earth by sending them to the grave at the same time. . . . Or, on the contrary, did Death try last year to favor *democracy* by destroying with the great names their authority as well and promoting intellectual equality? . . . Last year not a single king died. The gods are dying;—but we keep the kings.[23]

The real question that Heine posed concerned the political meaning of the loss of Germany's greats. As he put it, "Was respect or insolence the reason why Death spared the kings in the past year?"[24] Did the absence of brilliant representatives of German creativity simply make room for tradition, regardless of content—that is, for the kings to step in, become entrenched, and represent the German people and the German spirit? Or did it make room for the collective spirit of the people to express itself directly? Would a cult of genius, the veneration of lost genius, favor aristocracy or democracy?

These questions, so alive for Heine, and for Arnold Ruge as well, were more radical than, and yet related to, the popular debate about the cult of genius that occupied opinion makers like Menzel. The burning issue for much of literate Germany after the death of Goethe was not the appropriateness of the cult of genius itself but *who* were the appropriate objects of such a cult for contemporary Germany.

Genius and Political Tendencies

Menzel stood with Hengstenberg against the cult of the Weimar Olympian, but in contrast to Hengstenberg he espoused the form of the new religion described by Strauss as spreading like a miasma throughout Germany. Menzel's view is a prime example of that marriage between Romanticism and political liberalism solemnized by a multitude of Romanticists—old Germans—who had understood freedom to mean the external liberation of Germany from the yoke of France.[25] These men fought against foreign domination and a foreign system of thought in the name of a German self-identity that was to be found in its past or in its cultural products. But after the wars of liberation, these same Romanticists related liberation to the "domestic freedom of the nation, and took sides with the constitutional opposition."[26]

Yet Romanticism was also capable of a marriage with political conservatism. As Heine described it: "[At the time of the Freedom Wars] the Romantic School went hand in hand with the aims of the governments and the secret societies, and Mr. A. W. Schlegel conspired against Racine with the same objective as that of Prime Minister Stein when he conspired against Napoleon."[27] But "that school swam with the current of the time," and "the current was flowing back to its source."[28] Heine's reference is to the conversion to Catholicism of many of early Romanticism's leaders, including Friedrich Schlegel, and their subsequent support of the Restoration.

The result in literature of the marriage of Romanticism with political conscience was the triumph of the German-Christian-

Romantic school, the "neo-German-religious patriotic art." Yet as late as the 1830s, as Menzel pointed out, this type of art was not considered unequivocally supportive of the Restoration. He saw its fundamental dynamic clearly: "The more the old was destroyed, and continued to be destroyed in real life [by that trivial equality sought by the French Revolution], the more did the poets occupy themselves with grasping it in *its former completeness, as a perfect picture, with the first freshness of all its colors*, and comparing the contemptible reality with this beautiful ideal."[29] Yet the flaw in the present system evidenced by its paling against the glories of old obviously could produce two responses—a cooperation, like that of Schlegel, in the restoration of the immediate past or a fervor, like that of Menzel, to carry out the goals of the wars of liberation and reform the present toward the ideal of a truly united Germany with a constitutional government.

For Menzel, a creative artist, Friedrich Schiller (1759–1805), rather than popes and kings or knights of old, was a proper object for a cult of worship because in Schiller and the heroes in his plays was to be found the genuine German opposition to the destructive French spirit. He wrote: "In Schiller's ideas, we meet no dead mechanical law, no theory, no dry system of morals, but a living organic nature, a stirring life of active men. This ideal nature is the creation of genius."[30] In an encomium to such genius, the literary historian, ex–freedom fighter, marveled at men "whom no traditional measure fits, but with whom the world itself is born again. . . . This second birth is the work of genius." He also used the analogy for genius most dear to the ancestors of modern pantheism, who found God in nature: that is, the flower "existing only in a single specimen, wholly peculiar as to form, fragrance and color."[31]

The category *genius*, while correlative with the type of pantheism described by Strauss and Menzel and thus at home with the concept of a universal ongoing incarnation of the divine, also carried the meaning of uniqueness. This duality emerges in the way that Menzel transformed the individual character, Schiller, into the unique character of a people, the German people's latent "national genius."[32] He equated the morality, honor, action, and bravery of Schiller's heroes and of Schiller himself with what he saw as the virtues and potential of true Germany, its emerging middle class. In contrast to this, he disparaged Goethe's frivolity, arrogance, and lack of principle, which he identified with the character of the aristocracy blocking the unification of Germany and thus the achievement of its greatness.

The history of the concepts of the interchange between an individual genius and the character of a people in Germany is long and complicated. In the early nineteenth century there were those conservatives who argued in the wake of the Enlightenment and the French Revolution that the nobility, and ultimately the person of the king, is the genuine representative of the silent masses.[33] Early Romantics espoused a potentially competing concept: the representative powers of kings are limited to their age, while the true representative of Germany is poetic genius in touch with the universal qualities of humanity transformed into a specific national character.[34]

Essential to Menzel's association of the cult of Schiller's genius and liberal nationalism was his distinction between proper and improper, useful and untimely, forms of the characteristic German inwardness. He understood Goethe's form as improper, as ineffective egoism. Schiller and his characters, on the other hand, possessed "inner charm of soul." This "moral element" appears in the changes and the life of *history*; action, struggle, is "the sphere in which it moves."[35] In Schiller a genius with "angelic innocence" carried "a sword" and evidenced "every noble development of genuine manliness."[36] A proper type of contrasting genius is that of the artist Raphael, that is, "one that rests in the consciousness of a peace never to be disturbed."[37] But this type is untimely because of the need for models of action in history.

Distinctions between types of creative genius were not Menzel's invention. Rather, they were common in German literary history. Schiller himself, in *Naive and Sentimental Poetry*, had distinguished what he considered "a serenity and singleness of impulse" from his own sentimental creativity "arising out of an inner division of feeling."[38] This distinction is reflected in the contrast between early-nineteenth-century cultural ideals of "artlessness, effortlessness, continuing and profound inner harmony," on the one hand, and restlessness, energy, inner tension and an impulse to moral action, on the other.[39] Still another form of related distinctions was made by the poet and aesthetician Jean Paul (1762–1825), who contrasted feminine, receptive genius with masculine, expressive genius. The feminine genius is the one who has the capacity to take up the great world-spirit in a holy receptive soul but who cannot give adequate expression in language to this experience. This type of genius is in immediate contact with the unconscious and is at home with dreams, ghosts, and strange images.

The manifestations of such genius in Menzel's classification of German literature are most evident in the well-known tales of E. T. A. Hoffmann (1776–1822). The motivation for this type of literature, in Menzel's opinion, came from the romantic reaction against the modern spirit, as well as from a fascination with magnetism; its authors were those who took "a bold leap into the spirit kingdom" to meet the "demonic, the horrible, and the insane."[40] Jean Paul's masculine genius is also in contact with the unconscious, but can combine inner impulses with language by conscious manipulation and create an adequate product of expression external to the self.[41] In the second edition of his famous *Speeches on Religion to its Cultured Despisers*, Schleiermacher made a related distinction between the artistic genius who is silent, producing a work of art that is entirely internal, and the one who has an urge to self-expression.[42]

In the 1830s, Menzel popularized his own desired combination of these characteristics of genius. There is no doubt that for him masculine genius expressing itself in moral action was necessary for the times and was thus identical with the progressive German character. But his masculine genius did not battle against any inner tensions, only against external ones in the environment. For him, feminine receptive genius had become almost solely negative. While he did not deride peaceful genius like that of Raphael, Menzel left no doubt that a preoccupation with the inner self for its own sake was a force opposing progress. The type of "effeminate" genius like Goethe's not only retarded progress but also fostered a debilitating moral confusion.

Menzel was not alone in attempting to formulate a definition of the proper object for a cult of genius in the 1830s. Among Goethe's defenders, Strauss and Vischer identified the inner conflict of his characters as productive of irony, "the holy principle of spiritual freedom," that is, a principle of progress and reform.

The third edition of *The Life of Jesus*, with its genius Jesus, appeared in the context of this literary battle over the objects of the cult of genius. Strauss declared that such a cult was the only one that cultured people who were estranged from traditional Christianity could accept. In what he claimed to be an effort to show the relevance of Christianity to the present, he offered Jesus as the appropriate object of the genius cult.

What type of genius was this Jesus? What were the political implications of this type in the 1830s? As we will see, Strauss himself gave a full and direct answer to the first question. In order to provide a complete answer to the second question we will contrast the Jesus figure of the third edition with the portrayal of Wally by Gutzkow and then with Ruge's evaluation of this Jesus.

The Genius Jesus: A Justinus Kerner Figure

Strauss left no doubt about the type of genius to which the Jesus of the third edition belonged. He took great pains in "What Is Transient and Permanent in Christianity" to delineate that type, and in "Justinus Kerner" he attempted to defend its relevance for the Germany of his day. The Jesus of the third edition was placed among those geniuses whose focus is "the harmonious shape of the inner life" and whose very lives are "work[s] of art."[43] Geniuses of this type have such resources of soul, such richness and balance of talents, that even though they experience some inner conflict, as any human must, they have the capacity to overcome it without resorting to external mediation through objective formations. Such geniuses are contrasted with those who have the "impulse and call" to express, to present externally, what lies within them in "works of art or science, deeds of war or peace."[44] A certain tendency to neglect the harmony of the inner life, as well as a tendency to manifest one particular talent, such as "power of thought" or intense "imagination" or "practical understanding," more than others, marks these geniuses who are driven to externalization.[45] Inner piety, a true "piety of heart and sensibility," the subordination of all lower powers of the soul to the highest consciousness, marks the introspective class of geniuses to which religious figures like Jesus belong.[46]

It is obvious that this inward genius stands on the side of Jean Paul's feminine genius, Schleiermacher's silent genius, Schleiermacher's ideal of harmonious inner life, and even Schiller's naive Goethe. It has innocence of soul in common with Menzel's preferred genius, but little else, because this Jesus "belongs to an entirely different type [of genius] than all those whom world history praises as heroes of wars and government, science and art."[47] It is interesting, though, that Strauss, who was thoroughly familiar with Menzel's anti-Goethe, pro-Schiller polemic, seemed to make a concession toward Menzel's ideal genius by admitting that heroes of history can have harmonious souls, but souls not as harmonious as those who do not exercise some particular outstanding externalizing skill.

Those desiring liberal political changes in Germany demanded that German culture provide models for progress toward national unity and participatory governments like those of England and France. To this group, then, the type of genius Jesus offered by Strauss as an object for the veneration of the cultured would have been of questionable utility. Likewise, no such genius would be found in the pages of realistic novels that achieved the standard for depiction that Menzel and others thought necessary for the health of German consciousness, insisting, as they did, upon that balance between "internal character development" and "portrayal of the external world," which Frei argues is definitive of realistic narrative fiction generally.[48]

Yet even though geniuses of the interior life "as a rule do not enter into the historical progress of a people," they do have influence on humanity. They usually impress "a narrow circle of disciples with the soft whisper, the loving tones of inner disposition."[49] In giving an analogy for this type of influence, Strauss wrote: "In the quiet circle of families, the everyday interactions of civil life, that is where similar beautiful characters are found—as fathers, mothers, as farmers or traders, ministers or state officials, in each vocation and sex."[50]

It is clear that a Jesus who was such a "beautiful character" does not belong together with Caesar or Alexander or Napoleon. It hardly seems that this Jesus even bears comparison with Homer or Orpheus. He seems to belong in the company of quiet Pietists, to those who were at home in *Biedermeier* Germany. The morality of "true Germany," the solid middle class admired by Menzel and other south German liberals, was for them epitomized in the "sleepiness" of this genius Jesus. Yet even Menzel, who lauded such a morality, thought that class needed to be aroused from sleep into action. In other words, this religious genius could not provide a full cultural ideal consonant with political progress.

Moreover, other traits would make this type of genius ambiguous for the nineteenth-century political activist or even the noninvolved cultured person. Peter Hodgson pointed out that the Jesus who could be glimpsed in the first edition of *The Life of Jesus* was "religiously and philosophically inaccessible to the modern mind" chiefly because he understood his mission to be that of a principal in an imminent apocalyptic end of the world. In contrast, the Jesus of the third edition "understood himself in a strictly religious, non-political, non-apocalyptic sense."[51] But some curious aspects of Jesus' character—his working of some miracles, specifically cures, and his belief in angels and devils—appear in the third edition. Of these two oddities, the working of healing miracles should have been less troublesome to the educated nineteenth-century mind because of the upsurge of scientific interest in mental powers, in magnetism and hypnotism. However, since many of those who were apparently gifted with such powers seemed to "suffer from mental depression or illness," as Hodgson stated, to attribute such powers to Jesus was potentially to put into question his ideal mental equilibrium.[52]

To the nineteenth-century cultured person who would be asked to accept the genius Jesus, his first-century thought, or, better said, the limits of his thought, would be troubling. This was a level of thought in which objective reflection was shot through with unscientific imagery, what Strauss himself called "dross."[53] How could a person with this level of thought, such an eccentric, even if admittedly filled with piety, be an object of a modern German cult of genius? The answer to that question is given in the second of Strauss's *Two Peaceful Letters*, "Justinus Kerner," which appeared in the first issue of Ruge's avowedly Hegelian *Halle Yearbooks*.

Justinus Kerner (1786–1862) and the more famous Ludwig Uhland (1787–1862) were Swabia's prize romantic poets, characterized, as Menzel said, by the "vigorous and hearty simplicity of [their] genuine lyric poetry."[54] But he categorized Kerner not with Uhland but with the "effeminate" E. T. A. Hoffmann. He wrote:

> The mediator [between the side of darkened imagination and theology] . . . is Justinus Kerner, the amiable prophet of Weinsberg, whose friendly home among the luxuriantly trailing vines near the famous old castle "Weibertreue," is thrown open with the boundless hospitality to the dead as well as the living. . . . [His] activity as a magnetizing physician, which brought him into connection with the celebrated female seer of Prevorst, and with the spiritual world, has impressed the stamp of extraordinary peculiarity upon his literary works.[55]

Obviously, making Justinus Kerner better known to proponents of Hegel's philosophy, who made up the original audience for Strauss's article, would take a skillful hand. In fact, he made explicit his desire to show his Hegelian reader the kindness, love, and humanity of Kerner, to show them that if the poet did not transcend ghosts in his thought, he had done so in his humanity.[56] This is precisely the task Strauss had before him in the third edition: to show that if Jesus had not transcended the limits of his age in his thought, he had somehow done so in his humanity, or, more precisely, in his piety.

The first device that Strauss used to accomplish his purposes in the *Halle Yearbook* article was to begin with what was in effect a *Reisebilde*, a literary account of a journey.[57] He described a journey through space as well as time which he took in his own youth in 1827 through Würtemburg to Kerner's home to meet him and the seer of Prevorst, Fiederike Hauffe (1801–29), who lived in his house. He detailed a long, lulling trip through lush wine country alive with color and sounds as the practitioner of the newest philosophy prepared to meet the psychic-mystic-healer-poet who wrote peculiar poetry. There is a "suspension of disbelief" asked of the reader, who is in a sense being invited to see what is natural in another world.

In that world of southern Germany, Strauss, differing from Menzel, placed Kerner with Uhland, naming their poetic impulses as romantic, that is, as a "desire for the infinite."[58] Uhland and Kerner shared this fundamentally religious romantic impulse, but they differed in the way they expressed it poetically. Uhland made an attempt to locate the infinite in the finite, and thus his poetry focused intensely on finite objects and distinct, real human situations. Kerner, on the other hand, made an attempt to go "directly into the infinite," and as a result, felt the need to populate that infinity with imaginary figures, with ghosts. Strauss speculated that Kerner had actual visions of ghosts brought on by nerves excited by "the strength of his poetic impulse."[59] Here is a correlation between intense inner feeling of the desire for union with the infinite and disease which is not portrayed as illness. Thus, the intensity of soul capable of producing unusual effects on persons and things outside the self, possessed by Jesus as miracle worker and Kerner as healer, need not be viewed as an aberration of humanity but rather as a product of genius itself.

Moreover, Strauss explained that belief in ghosts and strange supernatural creatures is natural not only to humans at certain stages of history but also to humans with certain types of dispositions. A human who, whether because of the lack of progress of science or of inner intensity of soul, cannot appreciate the presence of the infinite in the finite, will, to possess infinity, "naturally" project finite objects into the beyond in order to assuage the inevitable pain and unhappiness of an empty infinity.[60] For a time, when "a spirit world with living shapes emerges from the formless mist," so that the beyond appears to have "determined laws and an actual influence on human life," the human feels satisfaction.[61] Soon, however, the figures come into focus, and their finitude, their incapacity to bear infinite content, is revealed.

This revelation of the finitude of supernatural creatures is similar to the dissolution of Greek religion and art in comic irony described in Hegel's *Phenomenology* discussed above. In fact, Strauss, although saying nothing about Hegel's philosophy directly, in effect criticizes Kerner for not responding in a Hegelian way to the inevitable revelation of the incapacity of the finite creatures of his imagination to bear the infinite content he desired of them. The proper response, according to Strauss, is comedy, in which the poet who created the supernatural creatures allows them to "bounce in the air for the delight of the viewer," held in mid-air between "the rationality of true consciousness" and the desired infinity.[62]

In his most devasting criticism of Kerner, and, in fact, in one of the most devastating attacks on the inadequacy of a post-Enlightenment stance of simple piety, Strauss bemoaned the fact that the poet not only is unable to allow for this type of comedy but goes so far as to ridicule reason. Kerner, who cannot do anything to forestall the recognition of the inadequacy of his supernatural creatures, attempts to overcome the effects of this recognition by ridiculing the enlightened person's lack of capacity to believe in them. In other words, the poet attacks reason. This amounts to a "self-sublation of irony," which itself leads to a sort of absolute pain because it takes away even the hope that the infinite can have content while still demanding that humans believe in it.[63] In essence, Strauss names the despisers of reason as the source of a potential existential despair. A Hegelian, on the contrary, respected reason and was convinced that the infinite does have content, *rational* content, that is "revealed" through the development, not repression, of scientific thought.

This stark analysis of the destructive potential of the romantic religious impulse is, however, almost an aside in Strauss's defense of Kerner, just as are his comments on the limitation of Jesus' thought in the third edition. It is overshadowed by his stress on the other possible product of a romantic desire for the infinite which attempts to go directly over into it—a poetry of harmony. This poetry is characterized not by the frustrations and despair of yearning but by themes of innocence, freedom from the complexities and temptations of society, and closeness to the healing powers of nature. A typical example of Kerner's poetry in this vein is: "O nature, if only I could be free of all human desires / and remain a child in your bosom."[64] Kerner's poetry conveys the quiet, peaceful, nearly satisfied realization of this desire. The Jesus of the third edition embodies this theme of Kerner's poetry; he remains the ever-loving child of the Father, close to the bosom of nature—the infinite.[65] Strauss maintained that innocence or absolute perfection was unattainable by any human, yet approximation to perfect union with the infinite, as Kerner's poetry illustrated, was a possible human attainment. This romantic religious poetry demonstrates then how it is relevant for the cultured modern German to conceive of Jesus "as the one in whose self-consciousness the unity of the divine and human first appeared with the sufficient energy to reduce to a disappearing minimum all the hindrances of this unity in the whole range of his soul and life."[66]

Yet the excellence of Kerner's poetry of harmony could not totally account for the poet's exemplary humanity. It was as though Strauss could not himself shake off the effect of the strange creatures of Kerner's imagination, just as in the third edition he could not shake off his conviction that Jesus' lack of the faculty of speculative reason qualified the definitive exemplariness of his humanity for Christians.[67] In the article on Kerner, he tried to vitiate this reservation with the hermeneutical principle that the man could not be fully understood from his poetry because his words could not and did not express the complete essence of his being. Some other sort of knowledge was needed. In Kerner's case, "when one knew him personally and entered his home," one could have no doubts that he was a warm, loving, outgoing, charismatic person.[68] In the third edition of *The Life of Jesus* there is a strikingly similar hermeneutical position. The personal experience of Jesus as the ideal of religious life is offered as the only proof of his definitiveness.

Strauss ended his defense of Kerner with a statement that in the hands of Heine might have reached the heights of irony, but which conveyed another mood in this defense of pathos. He wrote that when one had entered the home and personal circle of Kerner, the strange and potentially painful spirit creatures of his poetry seemed as domesticated as cats and dogs.[69]

There is a dramatic difference between the political implication of the first edition of *The Life of Jesus* and the third edition's affinity with *Biedermeier* scenes of domestic contentment with faithful dogs and cats. A comparison of Jesus as the ideal of inner life, who was lauded in this edition, with Wally should make this difference obvious.

Wally the Skeptic and Progressive Pathology

Wally is a counterfigure to rosy-cheeked female models of *Biedermeier* contentment, to the gentle genius of Kerner, who was at home in that environment, and to the genius Jesus. As we have seen, it is likely that Gutzkow was inspired by the death of Charlotte Stieglitz to create the portrait of Wally. To him and his fellow Young Germans, as Leo Löwenthal stated, "Charlotte seemed to be a type of human, who desired to liberate the middle class from the limits of . . . *Biedermeier* resignation into a conscious energetic life."[70] In other words, Wally was to arouse Germany from its sleep, just as Charlotte had intended to arouse her husband's dormant genius.

At the beginning of the novel, Wally is depicted sitting in her room looking at the works of Swabian poets: "These silvan poets take the liberty of being very *ennuyant*, she muttered. If their rhymes did not hold us in a kind of melodic suspense, the monotony of their feeling and views would be deadly. I prefer prose. Heine's prose pleases me more than Uhland and his whole coterie of bards."[71]

Like so many figures in German literature, and as Strauss tells us he did in his defense of Kerner, Wally takes a journey to a small village. She goes with her aunt to Schwalbach, a spa where she becomes depressed. In her case, geography fails to make conceivable another world view. In an effort to raise her spirits, Caesar tells her tales drawn from the local folklore. Wally reacts: "Go on with your drums and trumpets! What crazy things you get involved in."[72] Her mild distaste for being distracted by fanciful stories becomes horror when she discovers that Caesar's tales are unfinished. Their heroines are revealed to be real; they are women who end their lives and thus their stories by suicide while Wally is in their village.

Wally's own death is brought on by the failure for her of the roles and devices of Romanticism and its corresponding form of Christian religiosity. The Jesus of the third edition, as well as the poet Kerner, were characterized by their "inner harmony" of soul, by what was often called *feminine* genius. As a woman, Wally could be expected to have an innate gift for such genius.[73] But in contrast to the ideal feminine soul represented by Jesus and Kerner, Wally is torn by inner strife. In her case this inner strife does not set her apart as a driven genius as it might have. Because she lacks the resources given to men by their education, her inner strife merely becomes nervousness, disease. Wally suffers from "a religious tic": "Only in religious matters did she often pause. . . . Her brooding was unconscious, a dreary feeling to which she surrendered herself as she groped and tapped along. With Wally this could never have been the result of reflection, of logical investigations."[74]

Thus, rather than find romantic, cultural, and religious fulfillment, Wally has a religious problem. For example, she sees "mistakes" in the Bible, and she seeks rational explanations for the apparent irrationality of biblical narratives and dogma. But while she takes on the male prerogative of doubt, she is ill-equipped because of her lack of education to resolve it. She turns to the intellectual Caesar for answers, and he responds to her with an intensified skepticism, questioning even the most brilliant nineteenth-century attempts to reconcile reason and Christianity. Despite the depth of his own skepticism, however, Caesar is capable of being saved by femininity, by interiority, while Wally is not. In contrast to Wally, who cannot stop the thinking which gives her "a religious tic," Caesar's fiancée Delphine is one for whom "a certain undefined glimmer of feeling must be quite sufficient for her to sense the nearness of heaven."[75]

Wally is "terribly frightened by this plant-like unconsciousness in which women vegetate, this seeming fortuitousness of all ideals, attitudes and beliefs."[76] She writes of her envy of something close to what Menzel considered "manliness," that is, the ability to act:

> Men are lucky because demands are made of them. The measure of their actions is approval or the usefulness which they win. Tell me, too, why we shouldn't read *Faust*? The portrayal of the doubts that gnaw at a person's heart helps us understand him more and makes his effect less dangerous for us. But I feel that poems develop in every human soul, an entire chronicle of miracles which we despair of explaining, poems in which we ourselves are Ulysses, hunted by the gods, tormented, failing, erring. But this is only the half of it, you see. It's still not what I want to say and cannot say. Dear Antonie, that is the curse: nobody demands anything of us, nobody wants anything, it's not important at all.[77]

Delphine, on the contrary, is unafraid of being a woman: "Her love is quite plant-like in nature, oriental, as if contained in the hothouse of a harem that permits everything, every game, every feminine (but also sensually arousing) thoughtlessness, everything, everything—for that reason, Delphine is swollen with love."[78] She is perfect femininity in that she has, and wants, no will of her own, because her destiny, fulfilled with Caesar, is to come "under the protection of a man who is active enough intellectually to dominate her completely by means of his own strength of will."[79] In return, her absolute dependency and receptivity save Caesar from the pain of having to face the full ambiguity of his world.

Only Wally faces this ambiguity, suffering it in her failures to find love and her inability to obtain religious peace. In her, interiority, when directed toward the goal of passive receptivity, becomes true disease. Pathos with Wally becomes pathology. The novel presents an almost clinical description of her neurosis, which in turn becomes the vehicle for the depiction of a "diseased social organism."[80] For this disease there is no anodyne in interiority—no experienced presence of the infinite to resolve doubt and conflict.

In fact, the dynamic of the novel forces the reader to remain on the surface of Wally's life, to remain with its ugliness and meaninglessness. She remains an ordinary shallow coquette. She has no depth to escape to inside, and she has no place to run to outside. She is a pathetic ordinary girl, no genius at all.

Even if she is not a genius, Wally's story takes the form of a novel characterized by pathos, an emphasis on subjectivity. Gutzkow took pains to state directly that the topic of Wally was not intended to be "an individual genius," in the sense of one person's unique subjectivity, but rather an idea which was "given a penetrating examination under its actual conditions."[81] Leo Löwenthal has maintained that by *idea* Gutzkow meant the "powers of social organization in his day"—specifically, those of the middle class—and that by the *penetrating examination* he meant "a revelation of the inner divisions of that society."[82] In other words, in depicting Wally's inner life as marked by "pathology" rather than harmonious genius he provided a pathology of society, an image of a diseased social organism that could find no anodyne in tales of past glory or in interiority. The novel achieves this "sociological objectivity" through a "reversal of romanticism," through "a secularization, . . . a realistic-scientific analysis, a dissection, of the romantics' favorite configurations."[83]

The first edition of *The Life of Jesus* was also "realistic-scientific analysis," a historical investigation that without mercy "dissected" Christians' "favorite configurations." It achieved a secularization of Christianity in the sense that it portrayed the power of this absolute religion as belonging to the world, to "natural" human development, and not to the realm of mystery, accessible only to the chosen or gifted few. No "doubt about doubt" weakened its assertion that the truth of Christianity was not to be found in interiority but rather in reconciliation with objective, speculative thought. Thus, the first edition of *The Life of Jesus* was, like *Wally*, rejecting the ideal of harmonious inner life. Moreover, it too brought to consciousness the image of a diseased social organism. While *Wally* presented this image through pathos deepened into pathology, *The Life of Jesus* evoked it by forcing a contrast between an "objective" truth of Christianity, its ideal truth, and the "subjective," diseased forms of Christianity that served to retard the progress of the spirit in the 1830s. The comic irony of *The Life of Jesus* produced a demand for the actualization of the holy principle of spiritual freedom similar to that produced by the tragic irony of *Wally* that refused pathos in favor of pathology.

The third edition of *The Life of Jesus* was marked by pathos, and as a consequence it destroyed the effect of irony. In striking contrast to Wally the Jesus of the third edition took the form of one of the Romantics' favorite configurations. To those on the political left, such a Jesus was "behind the times"—indeed, potentially reactionary.

The Cult of Genius and the Aristocratic Jesus

Ruge, whose political sympathies were on the side of Gutzkow and the other Young Germans, including Heine, did not unequivocally affirm *Wally the Skeptic*. As a Hegelian, he had difficulty understanding pathology as progressive. In his opinion, not just an exemplar of the inner harmony of the soul, such as the Jesus of the third edition, but any concentrated model of subjectivity was of questionable value as a cultural expression of genuine human freedom, that is, one actually realized in the structure of society.[84] He criticized *Wally the Skeptic* and other Young German writings for being merely a "continuation of the ironic, abstract, genial self-satisfaction of Schlegel's romanticism." Their works evidenced "an egoism of genial irony, that was neither beautiful, nor sentient, but abstract and one sided," and they failed to achieve depiction of "material nature, flesh and blood, reality" or even "a realizable ideality."[85] In these criticisms, Ruge stood in fundamental agreement with Strauss's own reservations about *Wally* and Strauss's evaluation made in the defense of the first edition that the danger of his age was oversubjectivity. Ruge named this subjectivist tendency of the age *pathos*, a term he, like Vischer, used pejoratively to connote an excessive emphasis on interiority, a lack of objective distance, and a consequent antihistorical tendency.

Ruge interpreted pathos as a result of an irony which misfires, which, after disdaining the given order in the name of the rights of subjectivity, becomes so caught up with its own emotionality that it "fixates the pathological 'I' with its loves and hates," granting the most limited and finite of given empirical reality infinite worth. But it is not merely the genius of the interior life, one locked in subjectivity, who is "out-of-date" for the political activists of the 1830s. Ruge saw the same logic that transforms irony into pathos operative in any cult of genius. Here the flaw lies in the structure of the relationship of a group or community to the founding genius. Such a relationship is called *feminine*. In this context feminine connotes an excessively passive dependency on the genius, who, as the group's authority and oracle, is the active element. The cost of belonging to a cult of genius, or to what Ruge also called "the aristocracy of the gifted," is the loss of freedom brought about by the mandate for an unquestioning submission to the genius. Thus such a cult accomplishes exactly the opposite of what genius is thought to produce; it results in reaction, not newness and change. The reason for this is that the group affirms newness only as present in the genius, who by definition is different, separate, and exclusive. In Ruge's opinion, slavish, feminine dependence on an exclusive representative of the "new" is structurally the same as the unquestioning obedience to religious orthodoxy which supported reaction.[86]

Thus Ruge saw a potential in the category of genius for support of retreat from history. A genius or hero Christ would be acceptable if such a Christ were truly world-historical. But if a genius is to be one who moves the world, that genius must clearly be manifested as the expression for the spirit of the times and not "an arbitrary magician of the *Zeitgeist.*" World-historical heroes "are not Promethean bringers of fire who steal the truth from a transcendent heaven. They rather light the fire of truth which lies in the heart of the time." Heroes and geniuses can "take and give to us only what is already ours."[87]

This statement is in marked contrast to Strauss's discussion of world-historical heroes which he included in his defense of the Jesus of the third edition. He wrote:

> Two components can be distinguished regarding every genius and that genius's accomplishments—one personal and one historical. Each genius stands just as much on its own as it does on the shoulders of the past. In the final consideration, certainly, those geniuses living earlier in history, although having the same degree of personal endowments as those who lived later, are at a disadvantage. Those who live later in history have a richer inheritance from the spiritual progress of humanity which has grown greater and especially an inheritance from the masters of their particular talent. If the historical component of genius is related to the personal as matter to enlivening and ordering spirit, then it is clear that from a poorer and grosser matter, a spirit, although equally admirable with one who has a richer and more refined material with which to work, will not be able to form a body as splendid and beautiful as the other. This greater historical support, and not greater personal gifts, is what makes geniuses appearing later in history seem more admirable than those appearing earlier.[88]

Are the two components of genius described here the same as the two components of world-historical actions described by Hegel and espoused earlier by Strauss himself? Ruge did not think so. At issue is no longer the identity of the agent of historical change, whether it is the individual or the ethos, that is, the collective consciousness of humanity. Where there is a genius, the agent is clearly the individual who is compared to an enlivening spirit acting on matter. Moreover, although the agent cannot work without the matter, there is an element in the agent that is not truly in interdependence with the matter, the historical side. In this case, a subjectivity can be abstracted from this action of world history and admired, in a sense, for itself. This analogy of spirit and matter is used in the third edition to allow for the admiration of the genius of Jesus as having achieved the near perfection of inner harmony of soul beyond which no human living later in history would likely advance, despite the fact that other human activities, most importantly, speculative thought, had advanced. In his interpretation of the first edition, however, even in conceding that Jesus might have been admirable as a person, Strauss had drawn attention to Hegel's assertion that world-historical heroes are only fully understood as "the living instruments of what is in substance the deed of the world spirit," rather than in terms of their own personal uniqueness.

The apparently subtle difference between these two descriptions of historical agency was at the heart of the political radicals' experience of the ambiguity of the German cult of genius and of the theological Hegelian division into right, center, and left. The question is: Can a subject be isolated from the process of world history and worshiped and admired as an ideal of humanity? What are the political consequences of affirming such an isolation?

Ruge maintained that the individual in art or life becomes a figure of pathos when his or her subjectivity "freezes" by being cultivated for its own sake, and thus never attains objectivity. Similarly the group worshiping a genius becomes fixated on the genius for its uniqueness and can never attain true universality. Therefore, the Romantic, Pietist Jesus of the third edition, while apparently "liberal" because he is taken down from a heaven of divinity and placed alongside other human geniuses, is really a Jesus supportive of aristocracy.[89]

Thus the genius Jesus of the third edition tends to support an aristocracy of the gifted. The *true* Christ is not a genius, but rather "the sublation of the genius cult." The true Christ is the transfigured Christ of the first edition—the democratic Christ who grounds a spiritual democracy because he is present in the Christian community, "not as a privileged person, but as the shared holiness of all the community."[90]

Ruge's comparative reading of the first and the third editions of *The Life of Jesus* explains the political meaning of the two editions. The first edition portrayed the subject as real *only* in the collectivity, in a spiritual democracy; it removed the theological ground from the monarchial theory and from any Hegelian affirmation of a union of throne and altar. The third edition portrayed the subject as real in the individual, in the genius, who stands above others; it provided a ground for the legitimation of status differences between people and thus for an aristocracy and ultimately for a monarchy.

Chapter Six ❖ Political Meaning and Historical Effect

The purpose of this study has been to explain that the basis for the relationship between the definitive roles of *The Life of Jesus* in the history of Christian thought and in sociopolitical history is the text's political meaning. Like the novel *Wally the Skeptic*, the 1835 edition of *The Life of Jesus*, shaped by irony, conveyed a radical "consciousness of the abyss between theoretical idea and practical action."[1] Through the inversion accomplished by this irony, by which the historical individual Jesus Christ was replaced by collective humanity as the true subject of Christianity, the text depicted popular sovereignty as "the theoretical basis and ultimate culmination of the [religious] process," and thus implicitly of the political process.[2] In the language of the nineteenth century's most sophisticated defense of the vitality of Christianity in a post-Enlightenment world, the language of the Hegelian philosophy, *The Life of Jesus* concluded that the truth of God, of Absolute Spirit, in religion and in the state was to be found not in an individual but in a collectivity and thus in radical democracy.

In explaining the relationship between the roles of *The Life of Jesus* in the history of Christian thought and sociopolitical history, this political meaning also brings to light the necessity for a refinement of the definitions of these roles. Historians of Christian thought understand *The Life of Jesus* as the founding work of modern biblical criticism and as the work that crystallized the problem of believing in the truth of a historical religion in a secular age. Many Christian theologians focus on what they see as the text's unstinting affirmation of the rights of positivist historiography and its consequent misunderstanding of the potential of a philosophical hermeneutic, especially the Hegelian hermeneutic, to provide access to the meaning of the life of Jesus. From this perspective, the third edition is interpreted as a move in the correct theological direction. For their part sociopolitical historians, focusing on the text's inspiration of the left-wing Hegelians, describe it as contributing to the rejection of religion as a viable cultural force in the twentieth century. In *Political and Social Upheaval, 1832–1852*, William L. Langer gave a typical account of the reason for the political effect of *The Life of Jesus*. He wrote, "[It] did much to drain accepted faiths of their authority and to weaken the support which princes had derived from the Church."[3] In other words, the criticism of Christianity in *The Life of Jesus* undermined a religious faith that legitimated a political order, and thus it inspired and empowered the forces for change on the left.

Because neither the intellectual nor the sociopolitical historians have taken seriously the association between *The Life of Jesus* and *Wally the Skeptic* and thereby made the attempt to relate its theological erudition to the low-status naive knowledge represented by Wally herself, they have failed to attain that "historical knowledge of struggles" addressed by the text. Without this historical knowledge, aspects of the text's roles are lost. Along with the narrowing of the proper object domain that accompanies the division between the disciplines of history goes a narrowing of the concepts of historical causality. In this instance, the traditional explanations of the efficacy of *The Life of Jesus* in sociopolitical and intellectual history converge into a flat pattern: The text caused doubt about orthodox biblical faith, which in Christian thought shaped and stimulated biblical exegesis and hermeneutics and in sociopolitical history undermined political legitimacy. This study of the text as belonging with *Wally the Skeptic* suggests two refinements of that pattern which give it another dimension: first, the path *The Life of Jesus* took in contributing to the shape of modern history had two forks, one running through the political and theological right as well as one running through the left-wing criticism of religion; second, the left-wing criticism of religion is informed by the genius Jesus of the third edition and the pathos of interiority as well as by the irony and questioning of the status quo of the first edition.

In the decade after the appearance of *The Life of Jesus*,

discontent with economic and political conditions in Germany increased, until it emerged with full force in the revolution of 1848. In the aftermath of that revolution, proponents of broad-based representative government ultimately lost out to the forces of reaction, in fact, to the very advocates of Restoration, Hengstenberg and the Gerlachs, whom we have met as actors in the Pre-March. As Theodore Bigler put it, official German Protestantism, led by Hengstenberg, failed to "side with the people during [as well as after] the Revolution of 1848," with the result that eventually the German masses were alienated from the church and driven "to embrace the secular religions of Marxism and National Socialism."[4]

The Life of Jesus was no simple *attack* on faith, and its radicalism was not merely religious. It was a reinterpretation of Christianity and carried political as well as religious meaning in the Pre-March. Both of these meanings were immediately evident to those engaged in strengthening the union of throne and altar, as well as to those whom that union oppressed. Although the book did inspire those proponents of radical democracy who would develop modernity's most extreme criticism of religion, its equally significant immediate effect was to provide a rallying point for antidemocratic forces in Germany.

The immediate association between *Wally the Skeptic* and *The Life of Jesus* demonstrates that political and theological conservatives obtained in the theology text a perfect target for their attack against the forces of change. In virtually every issue of the *Evangelical Church Newspaper* from 1838 to 1848, Hengstenberg condemned *The Life of Jesus* or its author. Moreover, the division that *The Life of Jesus* made among theological Hegelians created the opportunity for Hengstenberg and his followers to discredit the potentially moderating influence of Hegelians in the Prussian government and to mount an attack on liberalism in all its forms in the name of protecting Protestant biblical faith.

Karl Göschel's criticism of *The Life of Jesus* illustrates well that belief in the personality of God and support for the unity of the state, as well as belief in the orthodox Christ and support for the hereditary monarchy, were held by the supporters of

Restoration to be intertwined. A divine order was called upon to legitimate the human order of the state. It would seem then that criticism of the Bible and Christian faith could create the potential for political change. Ruge, Heine, Marx, Hengstenberg, Menzel, and Göschel all recognized the potential political import of theological criticism. But did the criticism of orthodoxy in *The Life of Jesus* work solely or even primarily to create this potential in Pre-March Germany?

In answering this question in the affirmative, sociopolitical historians have overlooked what was so evident to the Christian theological historian F. C. Baur: a criticism of religion had taken place in Germany before the appearance of *The Life of Jesus*. Rationalist and liberal Christian theologians, affirming freedom of thought, had attacked traditional forms of biblical faith. By affirming freedom of thought, these theological positions carried the implicit political message of support for the rights of individuals to representative government. The works of such rationalist theologians as de Wette, Wegscheider, and Gesenius anticipated *The Life of Jesus* in becoming symbols of freedom of thought. Indeed, perhaps the most famous rationalist theologian still living in 1835, Paulus, joined Strauss as one of the few Germans to defend Gutzkow and *Wally the Skeptic*.[5]

But because Baur did not relate the repetition of theological tradition he saw in *The Life of Jesus* to such things as the rationalist Paulus's defense of *Wally the Skeptic* and thus to the general idioms of German culture in the 1830s, his knowledge of theological tradition has not been helpful to sociopolitical historians. Declaring that the text could not even claim the heritage of the Hegelian philosophy, Baur attributed its efficacy to the clarity and organization with which it repeated the rationalist theological criticism of the Bible.

What Baur and other intellectual historians fail to describe is that *The Life of Jesus* recast this German heritage of criticism of traditional Christianity in a politically subversive literary form, using successfully the culturally relevant language of Hegelianism, just at a time when the advocates of Restoration wanted Germans to forget that tradition, close their ears to the rumblings from the Paris revolution of 1830, shut their eyes, and go to sleep. *The Life of Jesus* disallowed that sleep, but in doing so not only with resounding clarity but also with contemporary irony it molded the tradition of theological criticism into a form which not only gave the politically discontent on the left a symbolic expression of the inversion of power they sought but gave the right-wing political and theological forces the perfect target for their invigorating attacks on the enemies of God and the state.[6]

It is not clear to what extent a victory of strong Christian theological rationalism or liberalism over Hengstenberg's neo-orthodox Pietism could have contributed to the victory of liberal politics in Germany. The categories of this type of theological position, which came to their most influential expression in Schleiermacher's thought, just like the categories of liberal politics, were drawn from the cultural expression of late-eighteenth- and early-nineteenth-century Germany. They held ambiguous political meaning. While capable of symbolizing freedom from the weight of historical tradition, they could also be read to support hereditary privilege in government. *The Life of Jesus* in its different editions forced the ambiguity of the German cultural heritage to the surface and provided grounds for both the forces on the right and on the left to oppose this heritage.

No Christian theologian or historian of thought has been more eloquent about the ambiguities of the German cultural heritage than Karl Barth. In what is probably the most influential article on Strauss in English, found in his history of Protestant theology in the nineteenth century, he drew a profile of Strauss as the epitome of the weakness of the liberalism in Germany. He recounts that Strauss himself was "deeply shocked by the revolution of 1848," that after the revolution he allied himself with the right in denouncing the actions of revolutionaries, and that finally he espoused listening to the genius Mozart as the ultimate religious act. Barth wrote: "And almost the last thing there is to be said about the nontragic quality of [Strauss's] general attitude . . . is that he did not even have the qualifications of a true evil heretic. It is that the result of all his negations was by no means an appalling Promethean uproar, but for all his attempted flat denials of God always only this self-conscious intellectual bourgeois quality, which was always morose, without the slightest notion of all the true heights and depths of life, the bourgeois quality in its specific national German form at the sunset hour of the age of Goethe, upon which Nietzsche then poured such cruel scorn as the embodiment of the 'philistine of culture!' "[7]

Those historians of Christian thought who comment on the cultural meaning of the 1835 edition of *The Life of Jesus* and who read it from the point of view of Strauss's intentions as gleaned from his biography or corpus, as did Barth, find it containing at least the seeds of "anonymous, flatly bourgeois morality."[8] Reading the text this way, they miss its political meaning of radical democracy which gave Strauss the status of a Satan, a "true evil heretic," to the right in the Pre-March. They fail to recognize the efficacy of *The Life of Jesus* to empower the right-wing defense of the personal God of the Bible, which it used to legitimate the monarchy. In the same way that sociopolitical historians can fall prey to oversimplification about the relationship between the criticism of Christian symbols and the destruction of political legitimacy without recognizing the dual route of influence of *The Life of Jesus*, Christian theologians and historians of ideas can fall prey to a naiveté about the multivalence of those symbols and the complexity of unambiguously claiming their content to critique culture.

Taking into account the left-wing Hegelian reaction to both the first and the third editions of *The Life of Jesus* also adds to the understanding of the dimensions of its historical effect. The discredit brought to the work by the third edition severely curtailed whatever part *The Life of Jesus* might have had in reshaping theological liberalism into a politically viable form for the young intellectuals of the 1830s who were seeking an effective contemporary expression of their ideas. This edition, with its gentle Jesus as a genius of the interior life, which formed a stark contrast with the collective Christ of the first edition, did indeed represent to the left the weaknesses in the German liberal theological and cultural heritage. This liberal genius Jesus was to the radicals a *Biedermeier* Philistine, an ineffectual figure who was manifestly "out of date" and retrogressive. Consequently, the 1835 edition of *The Life of Jesus*, in which Christianity was reinterpreted and not rejected as a positive force for transforming culture, lost its symbolic value for radical reformers. Members of the left-wing Hegelians went on to attack not just traditional forms of Christian belief as counterproductive to the development of modern humans but ultimately religion itself as destructive of human freedom.

Thus, because of the contrast it presented between its democratic Christ and the aristocratic-genius Christ of the third edition, *The Life of Jesus* of 1835 itself exposed what Barth called "the bourgeois quality in its specific national German form at the sunset hour of the age of Goethe." In the democratic Christ, in humanity as the miracle worker, the left-wing Hegelians identified a religious symbol with which to criticize a political authority legitimated by a form of Christian orthodoxy, a form which encouraged the misplacement of human potential in a figure of past history or in a heaven of resurrected bodies. These Hegelians left behind the religious and political viability of the democratic Christ when they became disenchanted with the aristocratic Christ. In rejecting this latter religious symbol, they were rejecting yet another form of Christianity, a heartfelt piety, which in Luther's Germany had often been deemed capable of freeing Christians from institutional and political contraints but which in the 1830s had developed negative political and social implications.

Neither the neoorthodox pietism of Hengstenberg nor the secularized piety of the antirevolutionary Strauss listening to the genius Mozart can explain fully the enervating effect of the aristocratic Christ on the left wing's enthusiasm for the democratic Christ and its consequent espousal of atheism. Only Wally's knowledge can explain it. Only Wally's attempt to escape the bell jar of German culture can reveal the pathology of heartfelt religion. More apt than any clinical description of this pathology is Wally's cry of fear of that "plantlike unconsciousness," of that seemingly infinite interiority that her religion and her culture designated as her proper realm. When read together with *Wally the Skeptic*, it can be seen that *The Life of Jesus* brought into question not only religion's potential to legitimate an oppressive political order but also its potential to create an entrapping inner space. The 1835 *Life of Jesus* caught up and changed the idioms of German culture to present an image of people struggling collectively for their freedom, an image which because of its capacity to call the status quo into question was associated with that of a Wally diseased and destroyed by her culture. The 1838 *Life of Jesus* offered the palliative of an aristocratic Christ, a genius Jesus, who was the epitome of the perfection of the inner life. Behind this image flickered that of Wally slowly and painfully losing her struggle for freedom in a boundless interiority.

What is "important" and "real" about *The Life of Jesus* is that it evoked these images of struggle.

Notes

PREFACE

1. This comment is from Linda Gordon's talk on the history of feminist theory delivered in September 1979. It is cited in the editorial statement of *Signs* 5, no. 3 (Spring 1980): 386.
2. Ibid.
3. LaCapra, "Rethinking," p. 271.

INTRODUCTION

1. Strauss, *Das Leben Jesu* (1835–36). Volume 2 bears the date 1836, but it appeared in October 1835. Volume 1 appeared in June 1835. For the sake of brevity, this title will be most often shortened to *The Life of Jesus*. The phrase *critically examined*, however, was essential in naming the book; a second edition appeared in 1837, and a third, importantly altered, edition came out in 1838. The fourth edition, which was much like the first, appeared in 1840. George Eliot translated this edition into English in 1846. In 1972, this translation was reprinted by Fortress Press, Philadelphia, with an editorial introduction and notes comparing the four editions by Peter C. Hodgson. Citations to this edition will be designated *ET*. References to the editorial introduction will read Hodgson, *Life of Jesus*. Where I quote passages from the first edition which were unchanged in the fourth edition, I use Eliot's translation with only minor stylistic revisions. When the passages do not agree, the translations are my own. These can be identified by the absence of a reference to the English translation.
2. LaCapra, "Rethinking," p. 271.
3. Recent bibliographies of Strauss scholarship can be found in Harris, *Strauss and His Theology*, and Sandberger, *Strauss als theologisher Hegelianer*.
4. See Droz, *Europe between Revolutions*, pp. 154–55, and McLelland, *Young Hegelians and Karl Marx*, p. 4.
5. Baur, *Kritische Untersuchungen*, pp. 46–47. This translation is from Harris, *Strauss and His Theology*, pp. 106–7.
6. LaCapra, "Rethinking," p. 249.
7. Barth, *From Rousseau to Ritschl*, pp. 362–89.
8. Gutzkow, *Wally, die Zweiflerin* (1835; reprinted, Göttingen: Vandenhoeck and Ruprecht, 1965). An English translation, *Wally, die Zweiflerin: Wally*

the Skeptic, by Ruth-Ellen Boetcher Joeres, appears in *German Studies in America*, no. 19. Page references here are to the English edition.

9. LaCapra, "Rethinking," p. 262.
10. Foucault, *The Order of Things*, p. xiv.
11. Foucault, *Power/Knowledge*, "Two Lectures," p. 81.
12. Ibid., p. 82.
13. Ibid., p. 83.
14. Ibid., p. 82.

CHAPTER ONE

1. Heine, "Concerning the History of Religion and Philosophy in Germany," in *Works*, p. 276. In its original form this essay appeared in a series of three articles published in France in 1834 in the *Revue des Deux Mondes*. The following year the articles were collected under the title *Zur Geschichte der Religion und Philosophie in Deutschland* and published by Hoffmann and Campe in Hamburg. This German version of the work was edited by the German censors. Mustard's translation, which will be quoted most often here, is from this German version.
2. Marx, "Zur Kritik der Hegelischen Rechts-Philosophie. Einleitung," p. 71. A translation of this article can be found in Marx, *Writings*, pp. 249–64.
3. This description was given by Ferdinand Christian Baur in a letter to a friend written in October 1836. This letter is cited in Harris, *Strauss and His Theology*, pp. 86–88.
4. See Wolfgang Menzel's review of *Wally the Skeptic* in *Stuttgarter Literaturblatt*, no. 93 (1835). His review of *The Life of Jesus* appeared in no. 100 (1836). This literary review was published by Baron Johann Friedrich Cotta in the *Stuttgarter Morgenblatt*. Cotta also published the *Allgemeine Zeitung* in Augsburg. His papers are considered to have been the most important in Germany in the first half of the nineteenth century. For a discussion of the importance of Menzel's *Literaturblatt*, the *Wally* incident, and Ruge's *Halle Yearbooks* in the history of the German press, see Ludwig Salomon, *Geschichte des Deutschen Zeitungswesens von den ersten Anfängen bis zur Wiederaufrichtung des Deutschen Reiches*, 4 vols. (Oldenburg and Leipzig: Schulzesche Hof and Hof, 1906), 3:487–502.
5. This letter, dated Christmas day, 1836, is in the Gerlach family archives at the University of Erlangen. It is mentioned in Bigler, *Politics of German Protestantism*, p. 178.
6. Krieger, *German Idea of Freedom*, p. 322.
7. Ibid., pp. 301–2.
8. Strauss, *Das Leben Jesu*, 1:v (*ET* p. li).
9. Ibid., 1:75.
10. Ibid., 1:2 (*ET*, p. 40).

11. Ibid., 1:vi (*ET*, p. lii).
12. Ibid., 1:vii (*ET*, p. lii).
13. Ibid.
14. Ibid., 2:736.
15. Ibid., 2:686 (*ET*, p. 757).
16. Ibid., 2:688 (*ET*, p. 758).
17. Ibid., 2:734–35 (*ET*, p. 780).
18. Ibid., 2:736.
19. Gutzkow, *Wally*, p. 30.
20. Ibid., p. 62.
21. This scene earned the novel a reputation as pornographic. Caesar convinces Wally to act the role of Sigone in the farewell scene from *Der jungerer Titurel*, a thirteenth-century work by Albrecht von Scharfenberg. The nude scene is described as though it were a medieval engraving.
22. Gutzkow, *Wally*, p. 108.
23. Ibid., p. 109.
24. For a discussion of the chronology of the compositions and appearances of these works see Schneider, "Gutzkow's *Wally* and D. F. Strauss's *Das Leben Jesu*," pp. 115–19. Late in his life Gutzkow wrote that *The Life of Jesus* had influenced him to write *Wally*, but as Schneider shows, this is impossible. Literary studies of *Wally* often repeat Gutzkow's erroneous comments.
25. See Dobert, *Gutzkow und seine Zeit*, and Dietze, *Junges Deutschland und deutsch Klassik*, for discussions of Gutzkow's intellectual biography.
26. Although this summary of Hegel's philosophy draws on his entire corpus, his writings on his overall system and on religion are most relevant. See especially, Hegel's description of the relation of his philosophy to idealist and romantic systems in his preface to *Phenomenology*, pp. 67–130. This work was first published in 1807 in Bamberg and Würzburg by J. A. Goebhardt. Citations here are from the Baille translation. Another translation by A V. Miller was published by Oxford University Press in 1977. For a more detailed discussion of these systems see Hegel, *Lectures on the History of Philosophy*, 3:252–89 on Spinoza, 3:423–78 on Kant, and 3:512–44 on Schelling. These lectures were given nine times from 1805 to 1830, and they were first printed as volumes 13–15 in *Werke*. Recent treatments of Hegel's stance toward these systems include: Fackenheim, *Religious Dimensions in Hegel's Thought*; Rosenstreich, *From Substance to Subject*; Efraim Shmueli, "Hegel's Interpretation of Spinoza's Concept of Substance," *International Journal for Philosophy of Religion* 1, no. 3 (1970): 176–91; Theunissen, *Hegels Lehre*; and Cornehl, *Zukunft der Versöhnung*. See Hegel, *Enzyklopädie*, no. 6. This work was first published in 1817 in Heidelberg by August Osswald's *Universitätsbuchhandlung*. And also see Hegel, *Lectures on the Philosophy of Religion*. Hegel lectured on religion at Berlin in the summer semesters of 1821, 1824, 1827, and 1831. These

lectures appeared as vols. 11 and 12 of Hegel, *Werke*. A translation of vol. 3, *The Revelatory, Consummate, Absolute Religion*, has been done by Peter C. Hodgson as *The Christian Religion*. Hodgson's discussion of the state of the German texts of these lectures (pp. vii–xxi) is excellent.

27. A thorough treatment of this position is to be found in Schleiermacher, *Christian Faith*, 1:3–93. Schleiermacher's original edition of this work was printed in 1821–22 by Reimer as the two-volume *Die christliche Glaube, nach den Grundsätzen der evangelischen Kirche im Zusammenhage dargestellt*.
28. Hegel, *Philosophy of Right*, p. 10. Hegel's *Grundlinien der Philosophie des Rechts* was published by Nicolai in Berlin in 1821.
29. Karl Mannheim, *Essays on Sociology and Social Psychology*, ed. Paul Kecskemeti (New York: Oxford, 1953), p. 132.
30. Ibid.
31. Hegel, *Phenomenology*, p. 79.
32. Hegel, *Philosophy of Right*, p. 218.
33. Marx, *Critique of Hegel's "Philosophy of Right,"* p. 24. This critical commentary on paragraphs 261–313 of Hegel's *Philosophy of Right* was never published during Marx's lifetime. It was written sometime between 1842 and 1843.
34. Strauss, *Streitschriften*, pt. 3, 95, 196.
35. Marx, *Writings*, p. 257.
36. Heine, "Religion and Philosophy," in *Works*, p. 364.
37. Ibid., p. 365.

CHAPTER TWO

1. Walker, *Germany and the Emigration*, pp. 47–51.
2. Ziegler, *Strauss*, pp. 68–69. The English translation here is from Harris, *Strauss and His Theology*, p. 26.
3. *The Hessian Courier*, distributed anonymously in 1834, was written by Friedrich Ludwig Weidig and Georg Büchner. This selection is from Büchner, *Plays and Prose*, pp. 169, 176, 177.
4. Bigler, *Politics of German Protestantism*, p. 267.
5. Quoted in Shanahan, *Conservative Phase*, p. 192.
6. Ibid.
7. Heine, "Religion and Philosophy," in *Works*, p. 276.
8. See Haller, *Restauration*.
9. Ruge, *Briefwechsel und Tagesbuchblätter*, 1:304.
10. Hamerow, *Restoration, Revolution, Reaction*, p. 4.
11. Büchner, *Plays and Prose*, pp. 175–76.
12. Harris, *Strauss and His Theology*, p. 5.
13. Slessarev, *Eduard Mörike*, p. 28. This poem is translated by Helga Slessarev.

14. Ibid., p. 26.
15. For example, the rationalist historian of the Bismarck regime, Heinrich von Treitschke, discussed Strauss under the rubric of "Young Germany" in the section of his work on the influence of French liberalism on nineteenth-century Germany. See Treitschke, *History of Germany*, 5:597–609.
16. Engels, *Schriften der Frühzeit*, p. 54. The English translation here is from Demetz, *Marx, Engels and the Poets*, p. 15.
17. Vischer, "Dr. Strauss und die Wirtembergers," col. 1120.
18. Immermann, *Werke*, vols. 3 and 4.
19. See Sammons, *Six Essays*, p. 128.
20. Heine, "The Romantic School," in *Works*, p. 180.
21. Quoted in Sammons, *Six Essays*, p. 127. The translation here is mine.
22. An excellent treatment of the political influence of this form of Christianity is found in Bigler, *Politics of German Protestantism*, pp. 88–124.
23. For a bibliographical discussion of the Awakening, see Erich Beyreuther, *Die Erweckungsbewegung, Die Kirche in ihrer Geschichte: Ein Handbuch*, ed. Kurt Dietrich Schmidt and Ernst Wolf, 4 vols. to date (Göttingen: Vandenhoeck and Ruprecht, 1961–), vol. 4, pt. R, sec. 1, pp. 1–4, 22–45.
24. Shanahan, *Conservative Phase*, p. 59.
25. Ibid.
26. Bigler, *Politics of German Protestantism*, pp. 183–84.
27. For a discussion of this dispute see Epstein, *German Conservatism*, pp. 128–45.
28. Ibid., p. 138 (emphasis added).
29. Ibid.
30. Rosenberg, *Politische Denkströmungen*, p. 23.
31. Ibid., p. 19.
32. Jaeschke, "Urmenschheit und Monarchie," p. 80.
33. See Hegel, *Philosophy of Right*, pp. 5–6. Hegel finished this work shortly after De Wette was dismissed.
34. See Lenz, *Geschichte*, vol. 2, pt. 1, pp. 172ff.
35. For an account of this incident see Bigler, *Politics of German Protestantism*, pp. 102–7. See also Gerlach, *Aufzeichnungen*, 1:180, for an account of this attack.
36. Ibid.
37. See Neander, *Erklärung*, pp. 4–8.
38. Quoted in Bigler, *Politics of German Protestantism*, p. 105.
39. Ibid.
40. See Jaeschke, "Urmenschheit und Monarchie," p. 80.
41. Ibid.
42. Ibid.
43. See Bigler, *Politics of German Protestantism*, p. 108.
44. Bretschneider, *Die Theologie und die Revolution* (Leipzig: F. C. W. Vogel, 1835).
45. For a discussion of this argument see Jaeschke, "Urmenschheit und Monarchie," p. 81.

46. Menzel, *Die deutsche Literatur*. This edition was translated into English by C. C. Felton as *German Literature*. The quotation here is from the English translation, 1:261.
47. For a discussion of the political importance of Hegel's philosophy in Prussia see Rosenberg, *Politische Denkströmungen*, pp. 69–77, and Gebhardt, *Politik und Eschatologie*, pp. 27–30.
48. Menzel, *German Literature*, 1:261 (emphasis added).
49. Schwarz, *Geschichte*, 1:9. Quoted in Harris, *Strauss and His Theology*, pp. 66–67.
50. Gutzkow, *Wally*, p. 87.
51. See the article by Werner Conze, "Adel, Aristokratie," in Brunner, Conze, and Koselleck, eds. *Geschichtliche Grundbegriffe*, 1:36–39.
52. Ibid., p. 39.
53. Hegel, *Philosophy of Right*, p. 176.

CHAPTER THREE

1. Heine, "The Romantic School," *Works*, p. 198.
2. On the meaning of Aristophanes in the Pre-March see Denkler, "Aufbruch der Aristophaniden," pp. 134–57.
3. See Hegel, *Phenomenology*, pp. 709–49.
4. Platen, *Die verhängnisvolle Gabel. Lustspiel in fünf Akten* (1826), in *Sämtliche Werke*, 3:267.
5. Heine, "The Romantic School," *Works*, p. 198.
6. Ibid., p. 199.
7. Löwenthal, *Erzählkunst und Gesellschaft*, pp. 102–3.
8. Gutzkow, *Wally*, pp. 38–41.
9. This secret report is quoted in Ruth-Ellen Boetcher Joeres's introduction to Gutzkow, *Wally*, p. 21. It is taken from Glossy, ed., *Literarische Geheimberichte*, p. 52.
10. Frei, *Eclipse*, pp. 211–12.
11. In this analysis, Frei uses the literary sociology of Erich Auerbach, *Mimesis: The Representation of Reality in Western Literature*. For other related discussions of this thesis see Watt, *Rise of the Novel*, and Sengle, "Der Romanbegriff."
12. Terry Hancock Foreman brought the importance of the limited political agency in disunified Germany to my attention.
13. Frei, *Eclipse*, p. 215.
14. For a discussion of this trend, see Wellek, *History of Modern Criticism*, 3:182–224.
15. For a discussion of the overall reaction to Menzel, see Dietz, *Junges Deutschland*, pp. 29 and 39.
16. This view was also held by Georg Gottfried Gervinus (1805–71), the other notable literary historian of the 1830s. Arnold Ruge also espoused

it. The correlation of literature with social and political life not only lent an impetus to the production of a national and nationalist literature in Germany but also contributed to what is now called the sociology of literature. At present, a concern with this correlation has come to the fore of German criticism. For a discussion of this trend, see Sammons, *Sociology and Criticism*; Jameson, *Marxism and Form*; Jay, *Dialectical Imagination*.

17. Menzel, *German Literature*, 3:276.
18. Ibid., p. 280. Willibald Alexis is the pseudonym of Georg Wilhelm Häring (1798–1871).
19. Ibid., pp. 277 and 280.
20. Ibid., p. 280. Frei, with many literary historians, relates history writing and narrative fiction. In his terms, they share "inseparability of subject matter from its depiction or cumulative rendering, literal rather than symbolic quality of the human subject and his social context, and mutual rendering of character, circumstance, and their interaction." Menzel definitely would have agreed with this but, as will be seen, he would have disagreed with Frei's assertion that miracles could receive realistic or "history-like" treatment if "they do not in effect signify something else instead of the action portrayed." See Frei, *Eclipse*, p. 14. See also Klaus Peter, "Wohldeuchdachter Radikalismus. Für eine neue Wissenschaft der Literatur," in Paulsen, *Der Dichter und seine Zeit*, pp. 33–52.
21. Menzel, *German Literature*, 3:284.
22. Ibid., p. 280.
23. Ibid., p. 54; see also pp. 3–55 and 1:213–78.
24. On the concepts of manliness and effeminacy in *Wally*, see M. Massey, "*Wally the Skeptic*: a Suppressed Feminist Novel," pp. 49–54.
25. Menzel, *German Literature*, 3:315–36.
26. See Sammons, *Six Essays*, p. 19.
27. Ibid., p. 121.
28. Wienbarg, *Zur neuesten Literatur*, p. 31.
29. Lukács, *Historical Novel*, p. 63.
30. Gutzkow, *Wally*, p. 110.
31. Ibid.
32. Ibid., p. 112 (emphasis added).
33. See Sammons, *Six Essays*, pp. 30–52. Sammons treats the issue of the realism of the Young German writings throughout his book and maintains that although the novels of this group are not comparable in form to those of the famous nineteenth-century realists, such as Dickens and Zola, the authors' intentions, as well as aspects of the novels themselves, move in the direction of this realistic fiction. Sammons also raises the fascinating question of whether the realistic narrative form does not inevitably tend toward conservatism in social and political perspectives and thus inevitably fail to express urgent and radical social and political criticism.

34. Although the topic cannot be pursued here, it is interesting to note that Strauss's and Vischer's discussions of irony as a mode of realism is similar to that found in an early (1920) work of George Lukács, *The Theory of the Novel*.
35. For discussions of German Classicism see Wellek, *Modern Criticism*, 1:12–30, 144–256.
36. Ibid., 2:318–24.
37. Hegel, *On Art, Religion, and Philosophy*, p. 29. The first volume of Hegel's lectures on aesthetics was published in 1835 by H. G. Hotho. This appears as volume 11 in Hegel's *Werke*.
38. Vischer wrote a response to and clarification of the introduction to Hegel's lectures on aesthetics in *Ueber das Erhabene und Komische*. See his definition of art, pp. 22–43.
39. See Wellek, *Modern Criticism*, 2:320. See also Morawski, *Inquiries*.
40. Vischer expressed his opinion on Menzel in a letter to Strauss (24 and 25 February 1837). See Rapp, *Briefwechsel*, 1:25–26. The *Turners* were followers of Ludwig Jahn (1779–1852), who was a leader in founding the *Burschenschaften* in 1815. The morals of the *Turners* would connote the binding together of the development of physical strength, devotion to religion, and patriotism characteristic of these *Burschenschaften*.
41. Rapp, *Briefwechsel*, 1:26.
42. Ibid., p. 21. *Philistine* was a term also used by Goethe and Schiller to connote a backward, conservative, and inartistic taste. The term was in common use in Strauss's day and could refer to almost any person or group that was viewed as nonprogressive.
43. Heine, "The Romantic School," *Works*, p. 211.
44. Hegel, *On Art, Religion, and Philosophy*, pp. 99–101.
45. Ibid., p. 98.
46. A similar interpretation of the late Hegel in the direction of the early *Phenomenology* (1807) was undertaken by Strauss in the third volume of the *Streitschriften*, addressed to Hegelian theologians. On this see M. Massey, "David Friedrich Strauss and His Hegelian Critics," pp. 341–62.
47. Hegel, *Phenomenology*, p. 709.
48. Ibid., pp. 709–45.
49. Ibid., p. 748.
50. Ibid., pp. 750–58.
51. Ibid., p. 758.
52. On the ambiguities of Hegel's treatment of art after the classical period, see Wellek, *Modern Criticism*, 2:320–21. Vischer's *Erhabene* is one of the first attempts to resolve this ambiguity of the place for "art" after the fulfillment of art.
53. Vischer, *Erhabene*, pp. 185–88.
54. Ibid., p. 187.
55. Ibid., p. 211. Hegel would have agreed that the Christian perspective on

the world is one of interiority. He defined the art of the Christian period of history as Romantic, in which subjectivity cannot find adequate sensuous expression.

56. Ibid., pp. 1–7.
57. See Wellek, *Modern Criticism*, 2:14–16, for a discussion of the interpretations of Schlegel's irony. It seems that Vischer here understands it as what Wellek calls objective irony, a form of paradox or "the simultaneous consciousness of the impossibility and the necessity of a complete account of reality."
58. See Strauss, *Streit*, 2:124, on *Wally*, and 136–77, on Goethe.
59. Strauss noted that theologians would probably find his criticism of Menzel to be a digression, but he maintained that there was a direct relationship between "charges of heresy in Christianity" and the condemnation of literature on moral grounds (see *Streit*, 2:92–93). Hengstenberg had also criticized Goethe for his immorality. See Hengstenberg's review of *The Letters between Goethe and Schiller* in *Evangelische Kirkenzeitung*, 1830, no. 10.
60. Strauss, *Streit*, 2:179.
61. Ibid., p. 180.
62. Ibid.
63. Ibid., p. 181.
64. Ibid., p. 184. As part of his criticism of Menzel's *Die deutsche Literatur*, Strauss wrote a defense of the Swiss historian Johannes von Müller (1752–1809), whom Menzel had compared unfavorably to the famous historian Justus Möser (1720–94), often called one of the founders of German historicism. What is interesting about this defense is that Strauss uses a historical method in the form of a somewhat detailed biography of Müller set in the context of concrete political conditions to affirm Müller's right to evidence the ambiguities of an appeal to national unity on the basis of a belief in a common German tribal root, an appeal that Menzel thought Möser had made and of which he approved (see *Streit*, 2:100–123). Here Strauss balanced character with environment.
65. Strauss, *Streit*, 2:185 (emphasis added).
66. Ibid.
67. Rosenberg, *Politische Denkströmungen*, p. 76.
68. Strauss, *Streit*, 2:181.
69. Gutzkow, *Wally*, p. 33.
70. Strauss, *Streit*, 2:186.
71. I would like to express my appreciation to Hans Frei for helping me clarify my terminology and mode of argumentation in this section and to Ruel Tyson for helping me ask new questions of Strauss's text.
72. Strauss, *Streit*, 3:136. See Karl Ullmann, *Theologische Studien und Kritiken* 3(1836): 770–816. Quotations here are from Strauss's citations in *Streit*. Ullmann affirmed the Christology and biblical exegesis of Schleiermacher, who also espoused a historical investigation of the Gospel but

asserted that such an investigation reveals the uniqueness of Jesus' personality, his perfect God-consciousness, as the originating impulse for the formation of Christianity.

73. See Strauss, *Streit*, 3:136.
74. Strauss, *Das Leben Jesu*, 1:375. Except for a few stylistic revisions this translation is that of George Eliot made from the fourth German edition (*ET*, p. 239). There are no differences between the first and the fourth editions in the passages cited here.
75. Ibid., 376 (*ET*, p. 240).
76. Ibid. Strauss himself reflected in the course of raising these questions that "it would occur to a cultured person that this account must come from a time when the home of the Deity was imagined to be above the vault of heaven."
77. Ibid., p. 381 (*ET*, p. 241).
78. Ibid., p. 381 (*ET*, p. 242).
79. Ibid., pp. 387–88 (*ET*, p. 245).
80. Strauss, *Streit*, 3:138.
81. Ibid., pp. 146–48.
82. Ibid., p. 150.
83. Ibid., p. 149. Strauss's own references are to Hegel's *Wissenschaft der Logik*, vol. 4 in *Werke*, pp. 185ff., and to the *Rechtsphilosophie*, p. 434. See Hegel, *Philosophy of Right*, p. 218. (Hegel's logic was first printed in three volumes in Nürnberg by Johann Leonard Schrag in 1812, 1813, and 1816.)
84. Strauss, *Streit*, 3:150–51.
85. Ibid., p. 151.
86. Frei, *Eclipse*, pp. 213 and 214.
87. Heine, "Religion and Philosophy," *Works*, p. 129.
88. Ibid.
89. Ruge, "Zwei friedliche Blätter."

CHAPTER FOUR

1. Jaeschke, "Urmenschheit und Monarchie," p. 104.
2. Gutzkow, *Wally*, p. 99.
3. Ibid.
4. Ibid., p. 97.
5. Ibid.
6. Strauss, *Das Leben Jesu*, 2:730 (*ET*, p. 778).
7. Gutzkow, *Wally*, p. 101.
8. Ibid., p. 106.
9. Ibid., p. 102.
10. Strauss, *Das Leben Jesu*, 2:732 (*ET*, p. 778).
11. Quoted in Löwenthal, *Erzählkunst und Gesellschaft*, p. 106.

12. Gutzkow, *Wally*, p. 106.
13. See chapter 2.
14. Gutzkow, *Wally*, p. 106.
15. Ibid.
16. Strauss, *Das Leben Jesu*, 2:729–30 (*ET*, p. 777).
17. Ibid., p. 730 (*ET*, p. 778).
18. Ibid., p. 731 (*ET*, p. 778).
19. Ibid., p. 732 (*ET*, p. 778).
20. Ibid., p. 733 (*ET*, p. 779).
21. Ibid., p. 734 (*ET*, p. 779).
22. Ibid.
23. Ibid. (*ET*, p. 780).
24. Ibid., p. 735 (*ET*, p. 780).
25. Ibid.
26. Ibid. (*ET*, p. 781).
27. See Bretschneider, "Erklärung," pp. 845–972.
28. Bretschneider, "Ueber das Verhältniss der Theologie und Philosophie unserer Zeit zur Sittlichkeit der Völker," *Allgemeine Kirchen-Zeitung* 15 (1836): 873.
29. See Jaeschke, "Urmenschheit und Monarchie," p. 84.
30. Stahl, *Philosophie des Rechts*, pp. 323–24.
31. See Jaeschke, "Urmenschheit und Monarchie," pp. 103–4.
32. Hegel, *Philosophy of Right*, p. 181 (emphasis added).
33. Marx, *Critique*, p. 27.
34. Strauss, *Das Leben Jesu* 2:734 (*ET*, p. 779; emphasis added).
35. Ibid. (*ET*, p. 780; emphasis added).
36. See Jaeschke, "Urmenschheit und Monarchie," pp. 83–85. In this context, the term *right-wing Hegelians* is restricted to the opponents of Strauss whom he actually names right-wing and thus to the actual historical participants in the debates over *The Life of Jesus* in the 1830s. Subsequent definitions of *right-wing Hegelians*, such as that of Peter Cornehl (in *Zukunft der Versöhnung*), which includes all Hegelian philosophers of religion who sought to maintain a continuity with the Christian tradition, obscure the historical situation. For example, Cornehl tries to show the correlation of a theological right with a reformist center political stance. Hermann Lübbe, in *Politische Philosophie in Deutschland*, also made this correlation. But as Jaeschke shows, neither Cornehl nor Lübbe deals with Strauss's actual right-wing opponents—among whom he named at "the most extreme right" Karl Göschel, along with G. A. Gabler and Bruno Bauer (see Strauss, *Streit*, 3:96). Bauer soon became a radical left-wing Hegelian, but in 1837 Göschel and Bauer were both extreme political conservatives.
37. Jaeschke, "Urmenschheit und Monarchie," p. 89.
38. Ibid., p. 90.
39. Ibid., p. 100.

40. Hegel, *Philosophy of Right*, p. 104.
41. This quotation is from Göschel's "Uber das Verhältnis der spekulativen Theologie zur Strauss'schen Christologie. Ein Votum zur weitern Ausführung," a portion of which is printed for the first time in Jaeschke, "Urmenschheit und Monarchie," pp. 85–88, 90–97. This quote is on p. 91. The original is in Altenstein's private papers. In 1838, Göschel's *Beiträge zur spekulative Philosophie von Gott und dem Menschen und von dem Gott-Menschen* repeats some of what is presented in the *Votum*, but the latter is much more explicit in its political purposes.
42. Hegel, *Philosophy of Right*, pp. 181–82.
43. Jaeschke, "Urmenschheit und Monarchie," p. 93.
44. Ibid., p. 94.
45. Ibid., p. 100.
46. See the discussion on the principle of analogy, pp. 28–29.
47. Jaeschke, "Urmenschheit und Monarchie," p. 82.
48. Menzel, *Stuttgarter Literaturblatt*, no. 94 (1835): 373. On this criticism, see Strauss, *Streit*, 2:212.
49. Menzel, *German Literature*, 1:261.
50. Ibid., 1:243.
51. Ibid., 1:259.
52. See the anonymously written "Dr. Wolfgang Menzel und Hegel," *Hallische Jahrbücher*, 1839, vol. 2, cols. 1489–1501.
53. Strauss, *Streit*, 2:204.
54. Ibid. See Hegel, *Science of Logic*, 1:60, and *Philosophy of Religion*, 1:114.
55. Strauss, *Streit*, 2:210. See Hegel, *Enzyklopädie*, sec. 564. See also Anselm K. Min, "Hegel's Absolute: Transcendent or Immanent?" *Journal of Religion* 65, no. 1 (January 1976): 61–89, for a recent treatment of the question Strauss addresses here.
56. Strauss, *Streit*, 2:210.
57. Ibid.
58. See Hegel, *Enzyklopädie*, pp. 456–61. See also the preface to the 3rd ed. (1830), pp. 23–28. George L. Kline, in "Some Recent Reinterpretations of Hegel's Philosophy," *Monist* 48 (1964): 41, gives a useful description of Hegel's use of the term *concrete* in comparison with the empiricist and ordinary use of the term. He said: "For Hegel, 'concrete' means 'many sided, adequately related, complexly mediated' (we may call this sense 'concrete$_H$') while 'abstract' means 'one-sided, inadequately related, relatively unmediated' ('abstract$_H$'). A concept or universal can quite sensibly be characterized as *concrete*$_H$, and at the same time, without paradox, as *abstract*$_E$, (the empiricist sense). Sense particulars, or 'sensuous immediacy,' will necessarily be *abstract*$_H$, and at the same time, unparadoxically, *concrete*$_E$." It is clear that here the "concrete unity" of God and humans refers to a unity which retains the integrity of its two sides, a unity which is "adequately related, complexly mediated." As will be seen, the empiricist sense of concrete as "sensuous immediacy" is described as the most "abstract" and contentless manner of perception.

59. Strauss, *Streit*, 2:214.
60. Ibid. The reference here is to Hegel, *Enzyclopädie*, pp. 8–10.
61. Ibid., 2:206.
62. Habermas, *Theory and Practice*, p. 175. Only a fragment of this essay exists. It is printed in Hegel, *Political Writings*. For another discussion of its place in Hegel's thought, see Avineri, *Hegel's Theory of the Modern State*, pp. 36–38.
63. Hegel, *Political Writings*, pp. 243–44.
64. Strauss, *Streit*, 2:206.
65. Ibid.
66. Hegel, *Philosophy of Right*, p. 198.
67. Strauss, *Streit*, 2:206.
68. See Hegel, *Phenomenology*, pp. 599–610.
69. See Hegel, *Hegel's Logic*, translated by William Wallace (Oxford: Clarendon Press, 1975), pp. 281–82. This is a translation of the first part of Hegel's *Encyclopedia*. On the concept of species, see Murray Green, "Hegel's Concept of Logical Life," in *Art and Logic in Hegel's Philosophy*, ed. Warren E. Steinkraus and Kenneth L. Schmitz (Atlantic Highlands, New Jersey: Humanities Press, 1980), pp. 121–50.
70. Strauss, *Das Leben Jesu*, 2:734–35 (*ET*, p. 780).
71. Ibid., 2:735 (*ET*, p. 780).
72. Ibid.
73. Marx, *Writings*, p. 402.
74. Strauss, *Streit*, 3:61–62 (emphasis added).
75. Marx, *Critique*, p. 39.
76. Strauss, *Streit*, 3:63–65. He comments that Hegel's criticism of Schelling is not as evident as is his criticism of Kant in writings such as *The Philosophy of Right*, *The Philosophy of Religion*, and *The Encyclopedia*. In Strauss's opinion, it is most evident in the preface to *The Phenomenology*, and he bases his analysis of the criticism on that preface, pp. 77–86. See also D. F. Strauss, "Vorlesung über Logic und Metaphysik," University of Tübingen, summer semester 1832 (Schiller National Museum, Marbach, no. 6826).
77. Strauss, *Streit*, 3:65.
78. Ibid., 3:66.
79. Ibid., 3:66–67.
80. Strauss referred to the conclusion of the first section of Stahl, *Philosophie des Rechts*.
81. Strauss, *Streit*, 3:57.
82. Ibid., 3:76–94. Drawing principally on *The Philosophy of Religion* and *The Phenomenology*, Strauss presents what he sees as apparently conflicting statements on what Hegel did think of the "historical [*historische*] validity" of the gospel history (*Geschichte*). Although he saw Hegel as leaving some questions unresolved, however, Strauss maintained that his philosophy did not exclude the free exercise of historical criticism. For a criticism of Strauss's use of quotations from Hegel in this section of the

Streitschriften see Theunissen, *Hegels Lehre*, pp. 240–42, and Sandberger, *Strauss als Theologischer Hegelianer*, pp. 120–21, for an opposing opinion.

83. Strauss, *Streit*, 3:58.
84. Ibid., 3:67.
85. Ibid.
86. Ibid., 2:37.
87. See Hegel, *Phenomenology*, pp. 93–94, 179–213.
88. Strauss, *Streit*, 3:68.
89. Ibid.
90. Strauss, *Das Leben Jesu*, 2:734 (*ET*, p. 779).
91. Hegel, *Philosophy of Right*, p. 104.
92. Marx, *Critique*, pp. 23–24.
93. Strauss, *Das Leben Jesu*, 2:734 (*ET*, p. 779).
94. Ibid., 2:735 (*ET*, p. 780).
95. Marx, *Critique*, pp. 24, 27, and 29.
96. Heine, "Religion and Philosophy," in *Works*, p. 339.
97. Ibid. (emphasis added).
98. Ibid., pp. 340–41.

CHAPTER FIVE

1. For an account of the changed reputation of Young Germany see Denkler, *Restauration und Revolution*, pp. 254–55.
2. For a discussion of the possible motives for Strauss's apparent compromise, see Hodgson, *Life of Jesus*, pp. xxxvi–xxxvii. "Zur Vergängliches und Bleibendes in Christenthem" appeared as part 3 of the first volume of *Der Freihafen* (Altona: J. F. Hammerich, 1838), "Zur Justinus Kerner" in *Hallische Jahrbücher* (1838) I, cols. 6ff. The two were revised and collected as *Zwei friedliche Blätter* in 1839. Citations to "What Is Transient and Permanent in Christianity," which was not substantially altered, will be from the 1839 edition. Citations to "Justinus Kerner" will be from the *Halle Yearbooks* version.
3. See Hausrath, *Strauss und die Theologie seiner Zeit*, 1:326–27.
4. See Ruge, "David Friedrich Strauss," col. 985.
5. On Strauss's initial role in the *Halle Yearbooks* see J. Massey, "*Hallische Jahrbücher*," pp. 42–68. Massey points out (p. 60) that in 1838 even Ruge was reticent to *directly* endorse Strauss's views in the first edition of *The Life of Jesus*. The journal's "boldest defense" came in September in an anonymous review of Strauss's *Polemical Writings*.
6. See Hodgson, *Life of Jesus*, pp. xxxvi–xliii, for a discussion of the changes in this third edition.
7. See Schleiermacher, *Christian Faith*, 2:413–71.
8. Schleiermacher gave these lectures at Berlin five times between 1819 and 1832. They were edited by K. A. Rutenik after his death and printed as

vol. I, pt. 6, of *Sämmtliche Werke*. These lectures, entitled *The Life of Jesus*, have been translated by S. MacLean Gilmour and edited by Jack C. Verheyden. See p. 124 of this edition for Schleiermacher's description of a creative artist. See also M. Massey, "The Jesus of History and the Christ of Faith."

9. Strauss, *Das Leben Jesu* (3rd. ed.), 2:771 and 2:778–79 (*ET*, pp. 799, 802; emphasis added). It should be noted here that since Schleiermacher's Christ bore characteristics of genius, Strauss's shift of position in the third edition has often been described as a move toward Schleiermacher. F. C. Baur had sent Strauss a criticism of his original *Life of Jesus* written by the mediating theologian Alexander Schweizer ("*Das Leben Jesu* von Strauss im Verhältnis zur Schleiermacher'schen Dignität des Religionsstifters," *Theologischen Studium und Kritiken* 10 [1837]: 502–6), in which the category of genius is discussed and to which Strauss seemed receptive. As we saw, Strauss took Ullmann, another mediating theologian, seriously enough to respond publicly and politely. In the third edition itself, he referred to Schweizer, Ullmann, and the Hegelian Julius Schaller as those who had urged him to consider the actual personality of Jesus as essential to his role as founder of a religion. See also Leander E. Keck's introduction to his translation of Strauss's *The Christ of Faith and the Jesus of History*, pp. lxiv–lxix.
10. Rapp, *Briefwechsel*, 1:39 (Strauss to Vischer, 21 August 1837).
11. Ibid., p. 40 (Vischer to Strauss, 6 September 1837).
12. Strauss, *Das Leben Jesu* (3rd ed.), 2:770–71 (*ET*, pp. 798–99). See Hegel, *Philosophy of Right*, p. 218.
13. See J. Massey, "The Hegelians," p. 119. This article gives an outstanding discussion of the left-wing Hegelian analysis of subjectivity. See also Frei, *Eclipse*, pp. 200–201.
14. Ibid.
15. Ibid., p. 123.
16. Ibid.
17. Strauss, "Vergängliches," p. 99.
18. Gutzkow, "Cypressen für Karoline [sic] Stieglitz," *Phönix Literaturblatt* 8 (25 February 1835): 189. Cited in Joeres's introduction to *Wally*, p. 1.
19. From Gutzkow's article "Vergangenheit und Gegenwart, 1830–1838," *Jahrbuch des Literatur* 1 (1838), pp. 72–73. Cited in Joeres's introduction to *Wally*, p. 15.
20. Kramer, "Ernst Wilhelm Hengstenberg," p. 135. Hengstenberg's review appeared on 11 November 1835 in *Evangelische Kirkenzeitung*, no. 90. See also Theodor Mundt, *Charlotte Stieglitz—Ein Denkmal* (Berlin: Veit and Company, 1835).
21. Strauss, "Vergängliches," pp. 99 and 100.
22. Ibid., p. 99.
23. Heine, "The Romantic School," *Works*, p. 180.
24. Ibid.

25. Menzel, *German Literature*, 3:200.
26. Ibid. Menzel further divided this group into "those who set out from old German reminiscences, from national feeling, and those who started from general ideals of freedom, and the dignity of many or from Schiller's point of view." He belongs to the latter group.
27. Heine, "The Romantic School," *Works*, p. 155.
28. Ibid.
29. Menzel, *German Literature*, 3:162 (emphasis added).
30. Ibid., p. 148.
31. Ibid., p. 149.
32. On this transformation see Pinson, *Pietism*, p. 178.
33. See Müller, *Die Elemente der Staats-kunst*; Stahl, *Philosophie des Rechts* II; and Friedrich Gentz, *Über den Unterschied zwischen den landständischen und den Repräsentativ Verfassung*. The Gentz text, written in 1819, can be found in Klüber and Welcker, *Wichtige Urkunden*.
34. See Forstman, *Romantic Triangle*, pp. 20–21, for a discussion of the views of Novalis and Friedrich Schlegel in 1798. In Schleiermacher's *Speeches on Religion to Its Cultured Despisers* (1799), he describes Jesus as this kind of representative or mediating figure. He wrote: "The truly divine is the remarkable clarity that the great idea he came to present developed in his soul—the idea that everything finite requires a higher mediation in order to cohere with the deity." This translation is by Forstman, *Romantic Triangle*, p. 78, from the first edition of the speeches, *Schleiermachers Reden über die Religion*.
35. Menzel, *German Literature*, 3:149 (emphasis added).
36. Ibid., pp. 150–52.
37. Ibid., p. 150.
38. Foreman, "Religion as the Heart," p. 62. See Schiller, *Naive and Sentimental Poetry*.
39. Foreman, "Religion as the Heart," p. 65.
40. Menzel, *German Literature*, 3:231.
41. See Wellek, *Modern Criticism*, 2:105.
42. Foreman, "Religion as the Heart," p. 88 (n. 32). It is interesting to note that Forstman finds the young Schleiermacher in the *Speeches* desirous of describing the religious consciousness as a passive consciousness, "a consciousness of being acted on," and thus capable of responding, as is the Christian, to "origins in history." See *Romantic Triangle*, p. 78.
43. Strauss, "Vergängliches," p. 111.
44. Ibid., p. 109.
45. Ibid., p. 114.
46. Ibid., p. 116. This statement closely approximates Schleiermacher's definition of Christ given in *The Christian Faith*.
47. Strauss, "Vergängliches," p. 118.
48. Ibid., p. 114.
49. Ibid.

50. Ibid., p. 115.
51. Hodgson, *Life of Jesus*, p. xl.
52. Ibid., pp. xlii–xliii.
53. Ibid., p. 801. See also Strauss, "Vergängliches," p. 122, and *Das Leben Jesu* (3rd ed.), 2:775 (*ET*, p. 801).
54. Menzel, *German Literature*, 3:248. On the poets Uhland and Kerner see Fröschle, *Ludwig Uhland und Die Romantik* and *Justinus Kerner und Ludwig Uhland*; and Straumann, *Justinus Kerner und der Okkultismus*. Straumann draws heavily on Strauss's 1838 article. See also Heizmann, *Justinus Kerner als Romantiker*.
55. Menzel, *German Literature*, 3:247–48.
56. See J. Massey, "*Hallische Jahrbücher*," pp. 44–47.
57. The autobiographical part of this article is used by Gotthold Müller in *Identität und Immanenz* to demonstrate his thesis that the young Strauss came to Hegel immersed in a southern German form of almost mystical pantheism and thus misinterpreted Hegel himself as a pantheist. However, Müller does not take into account the literary genre of the autobiography and the uses that Strauss intended to make of it in his defense of Kerner.
58. Strauss, "Justinus Kerner," col. 30.
59. Ibid., cols. 30 and 39.
60. This description bears similarities to Hegel's discussion of oriental religion in *The Phenomenology*, pp. 696–70.
61. Strauss, "Justinus Kerner," col. 39.
62. Ibid., col. 40.
63. Ibid.
64. Ibid., col. 38.
65. Nineteenth-century German romantic pietists mixed this metaphor.
66. See Strauss, *Das Leben Jesu* (3rd ed.), 2:778–79 (*ET*, p. 802), and "Vergängliches," pp. 130–31. Strauss states that it is *possible*, that is, *conceivable*, for other people to achieve what Christ did, and he dismisses the arguments for the necessity of any *one* person to achieve religious perfection. He says: "Religion has no need to engage in such brooding of the intellect" because nobody superior to Christ has appeared.
67. See Strauss, *Das Leben Jesu* (3rd ed.), 2:777–78 (*ET*, 801–2), and "Vergängliches," pp. 131–32.
68. Strauss, "Justinus Kerner," cols. 49–50.
69. Ibid., col. 49.
70. Löwenthal, *Erzahlkunst und Gesellschaft*, p. 90. See also M. Massey, "*Wally the Skeptic*: A Suppressed Feminist Novel."
71. Gutzkow, *Wally*, p. 32.
72. Ibid., p. 46.
73. The examples are everywhere in early-nineteenth-century German culture. Jean Paul himself had used the model of a loving wife to illustrate feminine genius. In lauding creative subjectivity, Friedrich Schlegel had

written the novel *Lucinde* (1799). Schleiermacher produced memorable images of ideal women in *The Christmas Eve Dialogues* (1805). This famous theologian had defended *Lucinde* six years earlier in a series of published *confidential* letters. The year before he wrote *Wally*, Gutzkow had published a new edition of these letters with an introduction in which he criticized *Lucinde*'s romanticism and abstraction from social issues. See Schleiermacher, *Schleiermachers Vertraute Briefe über die Lucinde*.
74. Gutzkow, *Wally*, p. 53.
75. Ibid., p. 85.
76. Ibid., p. 54.
77. Ibid.
78. Ibid., p. 85.
79. Ibid., p. 84.
80. Löwenthal, *Erzahlkunst und Gesellschaft*, p. 94.
81. See Gutzkow, *Ausgewählte Werke*, 5:89.
82. Löwenthal, *Erzahlkunst und Gesellschaft*, p. 94.
83. Ibid., p. 98.
84. See Ruge's review "Aristophanes Werke, übersetz von J. E. Droysen," col. 12. Ruge directly mentions only Mundt in this criticism, but his failures are taken as representative of the Young Germans in general.
85. Ruge, "Wilhelm Heinse's *Sämmtliche Schriften*," col. 1675. See also Eck, *Die Literaturkritik*, pp. 67–75.
86. Ruge and Echtermeyer, "Der Protestantismus und die Romantik," col. 427.
87. Ruge, "Zwei friedliche Blätter," cols. 1003–4.
88. Strauss, "Vergängliches," pp. 124–25.
89. Ruge, "Zwei friedliche Blätter," cols. 1003–4.
90. Ibid., cols. 1002–3.

CHAPTER SIX

1. Krieger, *German Idea of Freedom*, p. 322.
2. Ibid., pp. 301–2.
3. Langer, *Political and Social Upheaval*, p. 126.
4. Bigler, *Politics of German Protestantism*, p. 267.
5. See Dietz, *Junges Deutschland*, pp. 26 and 281 (n. 15).
6. See Gager, *Kingdom and Community*, pp. 37–48, 76–88, for a description of religion strengthening itself in the face of challenges to its claims. See also L. Festinger, *A Theory of Cognitive Dissonance* (Stanford: Stanford University Press, 1957).
7. Barth, *From Rousseau to Ritschl*, pp. 370–71. See Friedrich Nietzsche, *Unzeitgemässe Betrachtungen* (Leipzig: Fritzsch, 1873), p. 64.
8. See Hodgson, *Life of Jesus*, p. xxxvi.

Bibliography

Auerbach, Erich. *Mimesis: The Representation of Reality in Western Literature*. Translated by Willard Trask. Garden City, N.Y.: Doubleday, 1953.

Avineri, Shlomo. *Hegel's Theory of the Modern State*. Oxford: Cambridge University Press, 1974.

Barth, Karl. *From Rousseau to Ritschl*. London: S.M.C. Press, 1959.

Baur, F. C. *Kritische Untersuchungen über die kanonischen Evangelien*. Tübingen: L. F. Fues, 1847.

Bigler, Robert M. *The Politics of German Protestantism: The Rise of the Protestant Church Elite in Prussia, 1815–1848*. Berkeley: University of California Press, 1972.

Bramsted, Ernest K. *Aristocracy and the Middle Classes in Germany: Social Types in German Literature, 1830–1900*. Chicago: University of Chicago Press, 1964.

Brazill, William J. *The Young Hegelians*. New Haven: Yale University Press, 1970.

Bretschneider, K. G. "Erklärung über die mythische Auffassung des historischen Christus in Herrn D. Strauss Leben Jesu." *Allgemeine Kirchen-Zeitung* 16 (1837): 845–972.

———. *Die Theologie und die Revolution*. Leipzig: F. C. W. Vogel, 1835.

Brunner, Otto; Conze, Werner; and Koselleck, Reinhart, eds. *Geschichtliche Grundbegriffe. Historisches Lexikon zur politisch-sozialen Sprache in Deutschland*. 6 vols. Stuttgart: Ernst Klett, 1972.

Büchner, Georg. *Georg Büchner: Complete Plays and Prose*. Translated and introduced by Carl Richard Mueller. New York: Hill and Wang, 1963.

Cornehl, Peter. *Die Zukunft der Versöhnung: Eschatologie und Emanzipation in der Aufklärung, bei Hegel und in der Hegelschen Schule*. Göttingen: Vandenhoeck and Ruprecht, 1971.

Cromwell, Richard S. *David Friedrich Strauss and His Place in Modern Thought*. Fair Lawn, N.J.: R. E. Burdick, 1974.

Demetz, Peter. *Marx, Engels, and the Poets*. Translated by Jeffrey Sammons. Chicago: University of Chicago Press, 1959.

Denkler, Horst. "Aufbruch der Aristophaniden: Die Aristophanische Komödie als Modell für das politische Lustspiel im deutschen Vormärz." In *Der Dichter und seine Zeit-Politik im Spiegel der Literatur*, edited by Wolfgang Paulsen. Heidelberg: Lothar Stiehm, 1970.

———. *Restauration und Revolution: Politische Tendenzen im Deutschen Drama zwischen Wiener Kongress und Märzrevolution*. Munich: Wilhelm Fink, 1973.

Dietze, Walter. *Junges Deutschland und deutsche Klassik: Zur Ästhetik und Literatur Theorie des Vormärz*. 3rd ed. Berlin: Rutten and Loenig, 1962.

Dobert, Eitel Wolf. *Karl Gutzkow und seine Zeit*. Bern and Munich: Francke Verlag, 1968.

Droz, Jacques. *Europe between Revolutions, 1815–1848*. Translated by Robert Baldick. History of Europe Series, edited by J. H. Plumb. New York: Harper and Row, 1967.

Eck, Else von. *Die Literaturkritik in dem Hallischen und Deutschen Jahrbüchern* (1838–1842). Germanische Studien 42. Berlin: Emil Ebering, 1926.

Engels, Friedrich. *Schriften der Frühzeit*. Edited by Gustav Mayer. Berlin: J. Springer, 1920.

Epstein, Klaus. *The Genesis of German Conservatism*. Princeton: Princeton University Press, 1966.

Fackenheim, Emil. *The Religious Dimension in Hegel's Thought*. Bloomington: Indiana University Press, 1967.

Foreman, Terry Hancock. "Religion as the Heart of Humanistic Culture: Schleiermacher as Exponent of 'Bildung' in the 'Speeches on Religion' of 1799." Ph.D. dissertation, Yale University, 1975. Reprinted in University Microfilms, Ann Arbor, 1978.

Forstman, Jack. *A Romantic Triangle: Schleiermacher and Early German Romanticism*. American Academy of Religion Studies in Religion, edited by Stephen Crites. No. 13. Missoula, Mont.: Scholars Press, 1977.

Foucault, Michel. *The Order of Things: An Archaeology of the Human Sciences*. New York: Pantheon Books, 1970.

———. *Power/Knowledge: Selected Interviews and Other Writings, 1972–1977*. Edited by Colin Gordon. Translated by Colin Gordon, Leo Marshall, John Mepham, and Kate Sopher. New York: Pantheon Books, 1980.

Frei, Hans W. *The Eclipse of Biblical Narrative: A Study of Eighteenth and Nineteenth Century Hermeneutics*. New Haven: Yale University Press, 1974.

Fröschle, Hartmut. *Justinus Kerner und Ludwig Uhland: Geschichte einer Dichterfreundschaft*. Göttingen: Kümmerle, 1972.

———. *Ludwig Uhland und Die Romantik*. Cologne and Vienna: Böhlaw, 1973.

Gager, John. *Kingdom and Community: The Social World of Early Christianity*. Englewood Cliffs, N.J.: Prentice-Hall, 1975.

Gebhardt, Jurgen. *Politik und Eschatologie: Studien zur Geschichte der Hegelschen Schule in den Jahren 1830–1840*. Münchener Studien zur Politik. Vol. 1. Munich: C. H. Beck, 1963.

Gerlach, Ernst Ludwig von. *Aufzeichnungen aus seinem Leben und Wirken, 1795–1877*. Edited by Jakob von Gerlach. 2 vols. Schwerin in Meckl: F. Bahn, 1903.

Glossy, Karl, ed. *Literarische Geheimberichte aus dem Vormärz*, part 1: *1833–1842. Jahrbuch der Grillparzer-Gesellschaft*, no. 22 (1912).

Göschel, Karl. *Beiträge zur spekulative Philosophie von Gott und dem Menschen und von dem Gott-Menschen*. Berlin: Duncker and Humblot, 1838.

Gutzkow, Karl. *Ausgewählte Werke*. Edited by Heinrich Hubert Houben. 12 vols. Leipzig: Max Hesse, 1908.

———. *Wally, die Zweiflerin.* 1835. Reprint. Göttingen, Vandenhoeck and Ruprecht, 1965.

———. *Wally, die Zweiflerin: Wally the Skeptic.* Translated by Ruth-Ellen Boetcher Joeres. German Studies in America. No. 19. Bern and Frankfurt: Herbert Land, 1974.

Habermas, Jürgen. *Struckturwandel der Offentlichkeit: Untersuchungenen zu einer Kategorie der bürgerlichen Gesellschaft.* In *Politica: Abhandlungen und Texte zur politischen Wissenschaft*, edited by Wilhelm Hennis and Roman Schnur. Vol. 4. Neuwied: Hermann Luchterhand, 1962.

———. *Theory and Practice.* Translated by John Viertel. Boston: Beacon Press, 1973.

Haller, Karl Ludwig von. *Restauration des Staats-Wissenschaft.* 6 vols. Winterthur: Steinerischen Buchhandlung, 1816–1825.

Hamerow, Theodore S. *Restoration, Revolution, Reaction: Economics and Politics in Germany, 1815–1871.* Princeton: Princeton University Press, 1958.

Harris, Horton. *David Friedrich Strauss and His Theology.* Cambridge: Cambridge University Press, 1973.

Hausrath, Adolf. *David Friedrich Strauss und die Theologie seiner Zeit.* 2 vols. Heidelberg: Bassermann, 1876.

Hegel, G. W. F. *The Christian Religion.* Translated by Peter C. Hodgson. American Academy of Religion Texts and Translation Series, edited by James A. Massey. No. 2. Missoula, Montana: Scholars Press, 1979.

———. *Enzyklopädie der philosophischen Wissenschaften in Grundrisse.* Edited by F. Nicolin and O. Pöggeler. Hamburg: Felix Meiner, 1959.

———. *Grundlinien der Philosophie des Rechts.* Berlin: Nicolai, 1821.

———. *Hegel's Philosophy of Right.* Translated by T. M. Knox. London: Oxford University Press, 1952.

———. *Lectures on the History of Philosophy.* Translated by E. S. Haldane and Frances H. Simson. 3 vols. London: Routledge and Kegan Paul, 1968.

———. *Lectures on the Philosophy of Religion.* Translated by E. B. Speirs and J. B. Sanderson. 3 vols. New York: Humanities Press, 1968.

———. *On Art, Religion, and Philosophy.* Edited and introduced by J. Glenn Gray. New York: Harper and Row, 1970.

———. *The Phenomenology of Mind.* Translated by J. G. Baillie. New York: Harper and Row, 1967.

———. *Phenomenology of Spirit.* Translated by A. V. Miller. Analysis and foreword by J. N. Findlay. Oxford: Oxford University Press, 1977.

———. *Political Writings.* Translated by T. M. Knox. Introduced by Z. A. Pelczynski. Oxford: Cambridge University Press, 1964.

———. *Science of Logic.* Translated by W. H. Johnston and L. J. G. Struthers. Introduced by V. Haldane. 2 vols. London: Unwin, 1966.

———. *Werke: Vollständige Ausgabe durch einen Verein von Freunden des Verewigten.* 18 vols. Berlin: Duncker and Humblot, 1832–45.

Heine, Heinrich. *Selected Works.* Translated and edited by Helen M. Mustard. New York: Random House, 1973.

Heinzmann, Franz. *Justinus Kerner als Romantiker*. Tübingen: H. Laupp, 1908.
Immermann, Karl. *Werke*. Edited by Harry Mayne. 5 vols. Leipzig and Vienna: Bibliographisches Institute, 1906.
Jaeschke, Walter. "Urmenschheit und Monarchie: Eine politische Christologie der Hegelschen Rechten." *Hegel-Studien*, edited by Friedhelm Nicolin and Otto Pöggeler. Vol. 14. Bonn: Bouvier Verlag Herbert Grundmann, 1979.
Jameson, Frederic. *Marxism and Form: Twentieth Century Dialectical Theories of Literature*. Princeton: Princeton University Press, 1971.
Jay, Martin. *The Dialectical Imagination: A History of the Frankfort School and the Institute of Social Research*. Boston: Little, Brown, 1973.
Klüber, Johann, and Welcker, Carl. *Wichtige Urkunden für den Rechtszustand der Deutschen Nation*. Mannheim: Bassermann, 1844.
Kramer, Wolfgang. "Ernst Wilhelm Hengstenberg: Die Evangelische Kirkenzeitung und die Theologische Rationalismus." Dissertation, Friedrich Alexander University, Erlangen-Nürnberg, 1972.
Krieger, Leonard. *The German Idea of Freedom: History of a Political Tradition*. Boston: Beacon Press, 1957.
LaCapra, Dominick. "Rethinking Intellectual History and Reading Texts." *History and Theory* 19, no. 3. (1980): 245–76.
Langer, William L. *Political and Social Upheaval, 1832–1852*. The Rise of Modern Europe Series, edited by William L. Langer. New York: Harper and Row, 1969.
Lenz, M. *Geschichte der Königlichen Friedrich-Wilhelms-Universität zu Berlin*. 4 vols. Halle: Buchhandlung des Waisenhauses, 1910–18.
Löwenthal, Leo. *Erzählkunst und Gesellschaft: Die Gesellschaftsproblematic in der deutschen Literatur des 19. Jahrhunderts*. Neuwied and Berlin: Hermann Luchterhand, 1971.
Löwith, Karl. *From Hegel to Nietzsche*. Translated by David E. Green. New York: Doubleday, 1967.
Lübbe, Hermann. *Politische Philosophie in Deutschland: Studien zu ihrer Geschichte*. Basel: B. Schwabe, 1963.
Lukács, Georg. *The Historical Novel*. Boston: Merlin Press, 1962.
———. *The Theory of the Novel*. Translated by Anna Bostock. Cambridge: M.I.T. Press, 1971.
McLellan, David. *The Young Hegelians and Karl Marx*. London: Praeger, 1969.
Marx, Karl. *Critique of Hegel's "Philosophy of Right."* Translated by Annette Jolin and Joseph O'Malley. Edited and introduced by Joseph O'Malley. Cambridge: Cambridge University Press, 1970.
———. *Writings of the Young Marx on Philosophy and Society*. Translated and edited by Lloyd D. Easton and Kurt H. Guddat. Garden City, N.Y.: Doubleday, 1967.
———. "Zur Kritik der Hegelschen Rechts-Philosophie. Einleitung." *Deutsche-Französiche Jahrbücher*, edited by Karl Marx and Arnold Ruge. Paris: Bureau der Jahrbücher, 1844.

Massey, James A. "*Hallische Jahrbücher* (1838–1843): A Study in Radicalization." Ph.D. dissertation, University of Chicago, 1973.

———. "The Hegelians, the Pietists, and the Nature of Religion." *Journal of Religion* 58 (April 1978): 108–29.

Massey, Marilyn Chapin. "David Friedrich Strauss and His Hegelian Critics." *Journal of Religion* 57 (October 1977): 341–62.

———. "The Jesus of History and the Christ of Faith: D. F. Strauss's Criticism of F. D. E. Schleiermacher's Christology." Ph.D. dissertation, University of Chicago, 1973.

———. "The Literature of Young Germany and D. F. Strauss's *Life of Jesus*." *Journal of Religion* 59 (July 1979): 298–323.

———. "*Wally the Skeptic*: A Suppressed Feminist Novel." *Feminist Interpretations, Union Seminary Quarterly Review* 35 (fall and winter 1979–80): 49–54.

Menzel, Wolfgang. *Die deutsche Literatur*. 2d. ed. 3 vols. Stuttgart: Gebrueder Franckh, 1836.

———. *German Literature*. Translated by C. C. Felton from the 2d. German ed. 3 vols. Boston: Hilliard, Gray, 1840.

Morawski, Stephen. *Inquiries into the Fundamentals of Aesthetics*. Cambridge: M.I.T. Press, 1974.

Müller, Adam. *Die Elemente der Staatskunst*. Berlin: J. D. Sander, 1809.

Müller, Gotthold. *Identität und Immanenz: Zur Genese der Theologie von David Friedrich Strauss*. Zurich: EVZ-Verlag, 1968.

Neander, August. *Erklärung über meine Theilnahme an der Evangelischen Kirchen-Zeitung und die Gründe mich von der selben ganz loszusagen*. Berlin: Haude and Spencer, 1830.

Paulsen, Wolfgang, ed. *Der Dichter und seine Zeit-Politik im Spiegel der Literatur*. Heidelberg: Lothar Stiehm, 1970.

Pinson, Koppel. *Pietism as a Factor in the Rise of German Nationalism*. New York: Columbia University Press, 1934.

Platen, August von. *Sämtliche Werke*. Edited by Karl Goedeke. 4 vols. Stuttgart: J. G. Cotta, n.d.

Rapp, Adolf. *Briefwechsel zwischen Strauss und Vischer*. 2 vols. Stuttgart: Ernst Klett, 1952.

Rosenberg, Hans. *Politische Denkströmungen im deutschen Vormärz*. Kritische Studien zur Geschichtswissenschaft. Vol. 3. Göttingen: Vandenhoeck and Ruprecht, 1972.

Rosenkranz, Karl. *Kritik der Schleiermacherschen Glaubenslehre*. Königsberg: Gebrüder Bornträger, 1836.

Rosenstreich, Nathan. *From Substance to Subject*. The Hague: Martinus Nijhoff, 1974.

Ruge, Arnold. "Aristophanes Werke, übersetz von J. G. Droysen." *Hallische Jahrbücher*, 1839, I, col. 11.

———. *Arnold Ruges Briefwechsel und Tagesbuchblatter aus den Jahren 1825–1880*. Edited by Paul Nerrlich. 2 vols. Berlin: Weidmann, 1886.

———. "David Friedrich Strauss Zwei friedliche Blätter." *Hallische Jahrbücher*, 1839, I, col. 985.
———. "Wilhelm Heinse's Sämmtliche Schriften, herausgegeben von H. Laube." *Hallische Jahrbücher*, 1840, II, col. 1675.
——— and Echtermeyer, Theodor. "Der Protestantismus und die Romantik: Zur Verständigung über die Zeit und ihre Gegensätze. Ein Manifest." *Hallische Jahrbücher*, 1839, II, col. 1953.
Sammons, Jeffrey. *Literary Sociology and Practical Criticism*. Bloomington: Indiana University Press, 1977.
———. *Six Essays on the Young German Novel*. Chapel Hill: University of North Carolina Press, 1972.
Sandberger, Jörg F. *David Friedrich Strauss als theologischer Hegelianer*. Göttingen: Vandenhoeck and Ruprecht, 1972.
Schiller, Friedrich. *Naive and Sentimental Poetry and on the Sublime*. Translated by Julius A. Elias. New York: Friedrick Ungar, 1966.
Schleiermacher, Friedrich D. E. *The Christian Faith*. Translated by H. R. Mackintosh and J. S. Stewart. Introduced by Richard R. Niebuhr. 2 vols. New York: Harper and Row, 1963.
———. *Friedrich Schleiermachers Reden über die Religion, Kritische Ausgabe*. Braunschweig: C. A. Schwetschke, 1879.
———. *The Life of Jesus*. Translated by S. MacLean Gilmour. Edited by Jack C. Verheyden. Philadelphia: Fortress Press, 1975.
———. *Sämmtliche Werke*. 31 vols. Berlin: Reimer, 1834–64.
———. *Schleiermachers Vertraute Briefe über die Lucinde mit einer Vorrede von Karl Gutzkow*. Hamburg: Hoffmann and Campe, 1834.
Schlumbohm, Jürgen. *Freiheit—Die Anfänge der bürgerliche Emanzipation—bewegung in Deutschland im Spiegel ihres Leitwortes* (ca. 1760–1800). Düsseldorf: Pädagogischer Verlag, 1979.
Schneider, Franz. "Gutzkow's *Wally* and D. F. Strauss's *Das Leben Jesu*, eine Richtigstellung." *Germanic Review* 1 (1926): 115–19.
Schwarz, Karl. *Zur Geschichte der neuesten Theologie*. 4th ed. 2 vols. Leipzig: F. A. Brockhaus, 1869.
Sengle, Friedrich. "Der Romanbegriff in der ersten Halfte des 19 Jahrhunderts." In *Arbeiten zur deutschen Literatur, 1750–1850*. Stuttgart: Metzler, 1965.
Shanahan, William O. *German Protestants Face the Social Question*. Vol. 1, *The Conservative Phase, 1815–1871*. Notre Dame: University of Notre Dame Press, 1954.
Slessarev, Helga. *Eduard Mörike*. New York: Twayne Publishers, 1970.
Stahl, Julius. *Philosophie des Rechts nach geschichtlicher Ansicht*. 2 vols. in 3. Heidelberg: J. C. B. Mohr, 1830–37.
Straumann, Heinrich. *Justinus Kerner und der Okkultismus in der Deutschen Romantik*. In *Wege zur Dichtung*, edited by Emil Ermatinger. Vol. 4. Horgen-Zurich / Leipzig: Münster Press, 1928.
Strauss, David Friedrich. *The Christ of Faith and the Jesus of History*. Translated by Leander Keck. Philadelphia: Fortress Press, 1977.

______. *Das Leben Jesu, kritisch bearbeitet*. 2 vols. Tübingen: Osiander, 1835–36. 2d. rev. ed. 2 vols. Tübingen: Osiander, 1837. 3rd. rev. ed. 2 vols. Tübingen: Osiander, 1838. 4th. rev. ed. 2 vols. Tübingen: Osiander, 1839–40.

______. *The Life of Jesus Critically Examined*. Edited and with an introduction by Peter C. Hodgson. Translated from the 4th German edition by George Eliot. Philadelphia: Fortress Press, 1972.

______. *Streitschriften zur Vertheidigung meiner Schrift über das Leben Jesu und zur Charakteristik der gegenwärtigen Theologie*. Tübingen: Osiander, 1837.

______. "Zur Justinus Kerner." *Hallische Jahrbücher*, 1838, I, col. 1.

______. *Zwei friedliche Blätter*. Altona: J. F. Hammerich, 1839.

Stuke, Hans. *Philosophie der Tat: Studien zur Verwirklichung der Philosophie bei den Junghegelianers und den wahren Sozialisten*. Stuttgart: Ernst Klett, 1963.

Theunissen, Michael. *Hegels Lehre von absoluten Geist als theologisch-politischer Traktat*. Berlin: Walter de Gruyter, 1970.

Treitschke, Heinrich von. *The History of Germany in the Nineteenth Century*. Translated by Eden and Cedar Paul. 7 vols. London: G. Allen and Unwin, 1919.

Vischer, Friedrich Theodor. "Dr. Strauss und die Wirtembergers." *Hallische Jahrbücher*, 1838, I, col. 449.

______. *Ueber das Erhabene und Komische: Ein Beitrag zu der Philosophie des Schönen*. Stuttgart: Imle and Krauss, 1837.

Walker, Mark. *Germany and the Emigration, 1816–1885*. Cambridge: Harvard University Press, 1964.

Watt, Ian. *The Rise of the Novel: Studies in Defoe, Richardson, and Fielding*. Berkeley: University of California Press, 1967.

Wellek, Rene. *A History of Modern Criticism, 1750–1950*, 4 vols. New Haven: Yale University Press, 1955.

White, Hayden V. *Metahistory*. Baltimore: Johns Hopkins University Press, 1973.

Wienbarg, Ludolf. *Zur neuesten Literatur*. Mannheim: Löwenthal, 1835.

Ziegler, Theobald. *David Friedrich Strauss*. Strassburg: K. J. Trübner, 1908.

Index